ようこそ! ニッポンへ[改訂版]

── 映像で学ぶ大学基礎英語 留学生の日本文化体験 ──

Welcome to *NIPPON!*
[Revised Edition]
── Building International Friendship

JN112950

監修 田地野 彰
編著 石井 洋佑
　　 加藤 由崇
　　 中川 浩

朝日出版社

音声再生アプリ「リスニング・トレーナー」を使った 音声ダウンロード

朝日出版社開発のアプリ、「リスニング・トレーナー (リストレ)」を使えば、教科書の音声を スマホ、タブレットに簡単にダウンロードできます。どうぞご活用ください。

◉ アプリ【リスニング・トレーナー】の使い方

《アプリのダウンロード》

App Store または Google Play から 「リスニング・トレーナー」のアプリ (無料) をダウンロード

App Storeは こちら▶

Google Playは こちら▶

《アプリの使い方》

① アプリを開き「コンテンツを追加」をタップ
② 画面上部に【15682】を入力しDoneをタップ

映像・音声ストリーミング配信 》》》

この教科書の映像及び音 声は、右記ウェブサイトに て無料で配信しています。

https://text.asahipress.com/free/english/

Read, Think, and Write 執筆　Emily Snowden
映像撮影・編集／CPI Japan
イラスト (Words & Expressions)／Ayami Amy Ichino
イラスト (It's Your Turn!)／メディア・アート
表紙デザイン／大下賢一郎

は じ め に

　本書は、大学生にとってごく身近なトピックや日本の伝統文化や習慣を扱った映像教材を用いて、4技能のバランスが取れた英語運用能力の育成を目的として開発しました。授業では、映像の活用により、実際の場面・状況において学生が英語でのコミュニケーションを楽しむことができるよう工夫しました。

　本改訂版では、実際に教科書をご使用いただいた先生方や学生のみなさんの生の声を反映しました。たとえば、各Unitの最後にトピックに関連した読解素材（Read, Think, and Write）を追加することにより、聞く力と話す力はもとより、読む力と書く力のさらなる向上を目指しています。また、新たに各Unitダイアローグのスタジオ音声版やタスクのモデル会話を収録するなど、より幅広い指導・学習上のニーズに対応した教材となるよう改訂を行いました。

　英語が苦手な学生から英語上級者まで幅広い指導経験を有した英語教育の実践研究者たちが、異なる出身地の英語母語話者の協力のもと、指導経験から得た実践的知見と、それぞれが専門とする応用言語学・英語教育学からの学問的知見にもとづいて執筆しました。

　本書の特長と概要、構成は以下のとおりです。

特長

・魅力的な映像教材
　大学生にとってごく身近な事柄（アルバイトや買い物など）や日本の伝統文化・習慣を、映像を用いて視覚的に楽しく学ぶことのできる教材です。

・4技能のバランスのとれた英語力の育成
　具体的な英語の使用場面を意識しながら、4技能（聞く力・話す力・読む力・書く力）をバランスよく育成するためのバリエーション豊かな活動が掲載されています。

・英語に対して苦手意識を抱く学生にも最適
　英語が苦手な学生にも配慮し、細かな文法用語の解説などは省略し、さまざまな場面での英語の理解・産出に求められる表現と活動を導入しています。

概要

　本書は、アメリカからの交換留学生として来日したLauraが、留学先の友人Toruの助けを借りながら、さまざまな日本の文化や習慣を体験するという設定になっています。大学生活における二人のやりとりを通して、日本文化・習慣について考え、それらを自分のことばで発信するための英語運用能力を育成できるように工夫しました。

本書は 15 の Unit からなり、各 Unit（6 頁）の構成は以下のとおりです。

1. Watching the Video Clip (1st time)

まずは一度映像を見て、各 Unit の場面設定（例：道案内）を大まかに理解します。

2. Words & Expressions

イラストとともに、各場面での重要な英語表現を学びます。

3. Watching the Video Clip (2nd time)

もう一度映像を見て、より細かな場面設定を理解します。

4. Summary

穴埋め問題を完成させて映像の内容をまとめた文章を作ります。

5. Dialogue

ディクテーション課題を通じて、実際の会話スクリプトを完成させながら動画内容をより細かい部分まで理解します。

6. Useful Expressions

「意味のまとまり」ごとに語句を並べ替え、各場面で役立つ表現を学びます。

7. It's Your Turn!

実際の英語使用場面を想定したタスクを通して学びます。また、モデル会話を聞くこともできますので、活動後の振り返りなどに活用してください。

8. Read, Think, and Write

各 Unit に関連した読解素材を読み終えたのち、自分の考えを書いて表現します。

なお、今回の改訂版では発音関連の項目を巻末にまとめ、実際に映像教材で使われている表現を用いたポイント解説と練習問題を掲載しました。

映像に登場する Laura と Toru の会話を参考に、教室内での様々な活動を通して、実際に役立つ英語表現を楽しみながら学習してください。本書が、大学生一人ひとりの英語運用能力向上のための一助となることを願っております。

2021 年 9 月

監修者　田地野　彰

Contents

Unit 1 **Giving Directions and Helping** 3
● Target　道案内で使える英語表現

Unit 2 **Talking about Yourself** 9
● Target　自己紹介で使える英語表現

Unit 3 **Host Family** 15
● Target　留学生などを迎える時に使える英語表現

Unit 4 **Commuting by Train** 21
● Target　電車の乗換説明に使える英語表現

Unit 5 **Taking Classes** 27
● Target　物事の描写に使える英語表現 (1)

Unit 6 **Talking with a Teacher** 33
● Target　褒める時に使える英語表現

Unit 7 **Finding Friends** 39
● Target　自分の趣味や好みを伝える英語表現

Unit 8 **Potluck** 45
● Target　パーティーなどの集まりで使える英語表現

Unit 9 *Sumo* 51
● Target　物事の描写に使える英語表現 (2)

Unit 10 **Four Seasons** 57
● Target　好きな季節の説明に使える英語表現

Unit 11 Green Tea 63
◉ Target　物事の描写に使える英語表現 (3)

Unit 12 Japanese Food 69
◉ Target　料理の説明に使える英語表現

Unit 13 Part-Time Jobs 75
◉ Target　アルバイト先で使える英語表現

Unit 14 Shopping at a Clothing Shop 81
◉ Target　買い物で使える英語表現

Unit 15 Asakusa 87
◉ Target　オススメの場所を紹介する英語表現

Pronunciation

Consonants 1 (子音 1) 94
/b/, /v/ の違い・/f/, /h/ の違い・/ð/, /z/ の違い・/θ/, /s/ の違い

Consonants 2 (子音 2) 96
/r/, /l/ の違い・/m/, /n/ の違い・/tʃ/, /t/ の違い・/g/, /ŋ/ の違い

Vowels & Diphthongs (母音・二重母音) 98
母音 (vowels)・二重母音 (diphthongs)

Stress & Rhythm (強勢・リズム) 100
語内の強勢 (word stress)・文内の強勢 (sentence stress)・リズム (rhythm)

ようこそ! ニッポンへ [改訂版]

――映像で学ぶ大学基礎英語 留学生の日本文化体験――

Welcome to *NIPPON!*
[Revised Edition]
—Building International Friendships—

Giving Directions and Helping

ある日、Toru が買い物に出かけたところ、道に迷っている様子の女性 (Laura) を見かけました。Toru は声をかけてみることにしました。

Target 道案内で使える英語表現

Watching the Video Clip (1st time)

Task 動画を見た後、以下の問いに答えましょう。

Q. Which of the following sentences is true?

(A) Toru is a university student.

(B) Toru is saving money for Laura.

(C) Laura is looking for a library.

(   )

Disc 1
2))

Words & Expressions

Task イラストを見て、フレーズを完成させましょう。

1.

お手伝いしましょうか？

Do you need (h　　　　)?

2.

やがて横断歩道が見えます。

You'll find a (c　　　　).

3.

私についてきてください。

(F　　　　) me.

4.

右に曲がって、まっすぐ進みます。

(T　　　　) right and go straight.

Watching the Video Clip (2nd time)

Task もう一度動画を見て、以下の問いに答えましょう。

Q1. ストーリーに沿った正しい順番に並べなさい。

(A) Laura asks for directions.

(B) Toru says he can take Laura to Shonan University.

(C) Laura gets lost.

( ) → ( ) → ( )

Q2. What are Laura and Toru talking about?

(A) How to learn English

(B) How to get a driver's license

(C) How to get to the university

( )

Summary

Task 選択肢から適切な単語を選び、Summaryを完成させましょう。

Summary of the Dialogue

One day, Toru sees Laura struggling to get to Shonan University and asks if she needs [1]. He [2] her directions to the school, but Laura looks confused and says she does not [3] a good sense of direction. As Toru is a student there and has some time, he offers to [4] her to the university.

help	take	have	gives

Dialogue

 Task 🔳 もう一度動画を見て、以下の空欄に当てはまる語を聞き取りましょう。

Toru: Excuse me, do you need help?

Laura: Oh ... yes ... uh ... I'm trying to get to Shonan University. Could you tell me (1)[   ] [   ] get there?

Toru: Sure. Well ... how can I say? Can you see the street over there?

Laura: Uh-huh.

Toru: Go this way ... along the street.

Laura: Okay.

Toru: Then you'll (2)[   ] a crosswalk between a beauty salon and a restaurant.

Laura: Uh-huh.

Toru: Turn right and go (3)[   ] for a while ... and walk over the hill.

Laura: Um ... sounds very difficult. I have no sense of (4)[   ].

Toru: All right. Actually, I'm a student at the university, and I've got some time. I can (5)[   ] [   ] there if you want.

Laura: Oh really? That's so nice of you. You saved my day!

Toru: Don't mention it. All right, just (6)[   ] [   ].

Task ▨ 語句を並べ替えて、道案内で使える表現を英語で書きましょう。

※文頭の語句も、選択肢の中では小文字で記しています。

例 今、ここにいますよね。

[here / you / now / are].

だれが	する（です）	だれ・なに	どこ	いつ
You	are		here	now.

1. まっすぐ5分ほど歩いてください。

[for about five minutes / go straight].

だれが	する（です）	だれ・なに	どこ	いつ

2. 2つ目の角で、右に曲がってください。

[at the second corner / turn right].

だれが	する（です）	だれ・なに	どこ	いつ

3. 左手に公園が見えるでしょう。

[on your left / you / a park / will see].

だれが	する（です）	だれ・なに	どこ	いつ

It's Your Turn!

こんな時、あなたならどうする？

日本を訪れる外国人も増え、英語で道案内を求められる機会も増えてきました。ここでは、英語での道案内の方法を練習しましょう。

Task　Giving Directions

Q1. あなたは今、自宅 (HOME) にいます。自宅を出たところ、海外からの旅行者に最寄りのコンビニの場所を聞かれました。あなたは、以下のような地図を用いてどのように説明しますか？

Q2. ペアになり、質問役と説明役を決めましょう。

[質問役] 以下のような表現を参考に、地図上で行きたい場所を1つ決め、英語で尋ねましょう。
Hi, sorry to bother you, but is there a convenience store near here?

[説明役] 英語で相手の質問に答えましょう。

Sample Response

必要に応じて会話例を聞くことができます。

Read, Think, and Write

6 🔊 Task ▓▓▓ 以下の文章を読んで、設問に答えましょう。

Lost

Getting lost is common, especially when you are in an unfamiliar place. When you need to get somewhere on time, it can be quite frustrating. Luckily these days, most people have their smartphones, and you can usually get directions using GPS. Sometimes, however, GPS fails to connect. Also, you might feel more confused when looking at maps! Asking somebody for help is a simple solution. If you can find a person from the local area, then you're in luck! You will probably get the help you need. It will feel good to communicate with real people, too!

Although getting lost can be annoying, it can also be a positive experience. For example, if you're lost in a city, you might discover historical monuments, buildings, parks, and museums. If you're lost in the countryside, you might notice different kinds of wildlife. Getting lost can give you a chance to find and experience new things.

1) What is the passage about?
- (A) Asking for help
- (B) Getting lost
- (C) Trying something unfamiliar
- (D) Enjoying the local area

2) According to the passage, what can be positive about getting lost?
- (A) Being in an unfamiliar place
- (B) Asking for help
- (C) Finding and experiencing new things
- (D) Discovering new animals

3) Write about a time when you got lost.

Talking about Yourself

Toru は、大学までの道案内をしながら、Laura に自己紹介を始めました。そこで分かった二人の共通点とは？

Target 自己紹介で使える英語表現

Watching the Video Clip (1st time)

Task 動画を見た後、以下の問いに答えましょう。

Q. Which of the following sentences is true?

(A) Laura arrived at the airport this morning.

(B) Toru was born in the United States.

(C) Laura knows where Building 8 is. (   )

Words & Expressions

Task イラストを見て、フレーズを完成させましょう。

1.

自己紹介をします。
Let me (i   ) myself.

2.

私は交換留学生です。
I'm an (e   ) student.

3.

私はもともとニューヨークの出身です。
I am originally (f   ) New York.

4.

私は金沢で生まれ育ちました。
I was (b   ) and grew up in Kanazawa.

Watching the Video Clip (2nd time)

Task もう一度動画を見て、以下の問いに答えましょう。

Q1. ストーリーに沿った正しい順番に並べなさい。

(A) Toru will take Laura to Building 8.

(B) Toru introduces himself.

(C) Laura says she comes from America.

( ) → ( ) → ( )

Q2. Where did Toru study in the United States?

(A) Wisconsin

(B) Michigan

(C) Iowa

( )

Summary

Task 選択肢から適切な単語を選び、Summaryを完成させましょう。

Summary of the Dialogue

As they [1] to the university, Laura tells Toru that she is an exchange student and that she just [2] in Japan that morning from the United States. She thinks Toru has lived in the United States because he has an American accent. He says he [3] in Iowa as a high school exchange student. Laura says that Iowa is close to her hometown. After they arrive at the university, Toru [4] to take her to Building 8.

lived	arrived	walk	offers

Dialogue

 Task ▥ もう一度動画を見て、以下の空欄に当てはまる語を聞き取りましょう。

Toru: Let me introduce myself. My name is Toru Asano.

Laura: I am Laura Mueller. I'm an exchange student. Actually, this is my first day in Japan.

Toru: Oh ... you just arrived in Japan today?

Laura: Yeah ... I (1)[   ] [   ] Narita Airport this morning and I came here straight from the airport.

Toru: I see. So ... where are you from?

Laura: Well ... I'm (2)[   ] [   ] Wisconsin in the United States. But now I'm studying at a university in Michigan. How about you? You (3)[   ] [   ] in America or Canada, right? You speak English with an American accent.

Toru: Well, I was born and (4)[   ] [   ] in Tokyo, but I lived in the United States for an exchange program in high school.

Laura: Oh, cool. Which part of the United States did you live in?

Toru: I was in Des Moines, Iowa.

Laura: Oh ... Iowa! It's (5)[   ] [   ] my hometown.

Laura: Oh, is this the school?

Toru: Right. Do you know which building to go to?

Laura: Maybe ... wait ... it says Building 8.

Toru: No problem. I can (6)[   ] [   ] there.

Laura: You're so kind. I appreciate your help.

Task ▓▓ 語句を並べ替えて、自己紹介で使える表現を英語で書きましょう。

※文頭の語句も、選択肢の中では小文字で記しています。

1. 私は工学部です。

[of engineering / I / am / in the college].

だれが	する（です）	だれ・なに	どこ	いつ

注）1つのボックス内に入る語句でも、その語句を区切って選択肢に含めていることがあります。

2. 理学療法が専門です。

[major in / physical therapy / I].

だれが	する（です）	だれ・なに	どこ	いつ

3. 趣味はピアノです。

[playing the piano / my hobby / is].

だれが	する（です）	だれ・なに	どこ	いつ

注）だれが には生き物でないもの（無生物主語）が入ることもあります。

4. 卒業後は海外で働きたいです。

[would like to / abroad / I / after graduation / work].

だれが	する（です）	だれ・なに	どこ	いつ

It's Your Turn!

こんな時、あなたならどうする？

自己紹介はコミュニケーションの基本です。初対面の相手でも、落ち着いて自分のことを紹介できるように練習しましょう。

Task ▓▓ Introducing Yourself & Your Partner

Q1. ペアになり、自分のことを、あなたのパートナーに紹介してみましょう。
- ・名前
- ・学部（college, faculty）、学科（department）
- ・好きな有名人や趣味など

Q2. では次に、4人グループになり、あなたのパートナーのことを、クラスメイトに紹介してみましょう。
- ・パートナーの名前
- ・パートナーの学部、学科
- ・パートナーが好きな有名人や趣味など

Sample Response

必要に応じて会話例を聞くことができます。

Task █ 以下の文章を読んで、設問に答えましょう。

Third Culture Kids

Third culture kids are people who grow up in different places and cultures. They have backgrounds other than their parents' countries. They experience different cultures from around the world, and can often speak two or more languages. Third culture kids grow up learning about different points of view, and often have friends living all over the world.

To live in different places can be exciting, but it can also be a challenge. For many third culture kids, the challenge is to know where "home" is. So it is difficult to answer the question, "Where are you from?" For example, if you were born and grew up in Tokyo, you could just say "I'm from Tokyo." But it is not so simple for third culture kids. It can be difficult to feel connected to just one place and call it "home."

1) What is the topic about?
   (A) People with multiple cultural backgrounds
   (B) A conflict between two cultures
   (C) Learning a new language
   (D) The importance of friends

2) According to the passage, what is the challenge that third culture kids have?
   (A) To understand different cultures
   (B) To speak more than two languages
   (C) To experience life in different places
   (D) To feel connected to just one place

3) Do you feel "at home" where you live now? Why, or why not?

Host Family

Toruの手助けもあり、Lauraは大学での手続き
を無事に済ませた様子です。この後Lauraは、
どこへ行くのでしょうか。

Target 留学生などを迎える時に使える英語表現

Watching the Video Clip (1st time)

Task 動画を見た後、以下の問いに答えましょう。

Q. Which of the following sentences is true?

(A) Laura's host mother works at a hospital.

(B) Toru enjoys talking to Laura.

(C) Toru is going to meet his friend at the station. (　　　　　)

12 Words & Expressions

Task イラストを見て、フレーズを完成させましょう。

1.

私はホストファミリーの家に行く予定です。

I'm (g　　　　　) to my host family's
house.

2.

以前にホストファミリーに会ったことがありますか?

Have you (m　　　　　) your host
family before?

3.

あなたの連絡先を教えてもらって良いですか?

Can I get your (c　　　　　　)
information ?

4.

また連絡を取りましょう。

Let's keep in (t　　　　　).

Watching the Video Clip (2nd time)

Task もう一度動画を見て、以下の問いに答えましょう。

Q1. ストーリーに沿った正しい順番に並べなさい。

(A) Laura tells Toru about her host family.

(B) Laura and Toru exchange their contact information.

(C) Toru goes to the library to study.

( ) → ( ) → ( )

Q2. How many times has Laura met her host family before?

(A) Never

(B) Once

(C) Twice

( )

Summary

Task 選択肢から適切な単語を選び、Summaryを完成させましょう。

Summary of the Dialogue

Toru is [1] outside when Laura finishes her business, and they [2] a short chat. She tells him she is on her way to her host family's home, and that her host mother teaches Japanese at the university. Laura thanks Toru for his help, and they [3] their contact information. After they [4] to keep in touch, Toru goes to the library, and Laura heads toward the station.

exchange	have	promise	waiting

Dialogue

 Task もう一度動画を見て、以下の空欄に当てはまる語を聞き取りましょう。

Toru: Did you find everything OK?

Laura: I think (1)[   ] [   ]. Now, I'm going to my host family's house.

Toru: Oh ... you have a host family. (2)[   ] [   ] [   ] them before?

Laura: Not really. But ... my host mother is a professor at this university. She teaches Japanese to international students.

Toru: That's great! You can (3)[   ] [   ] [   ] about Japan from her.

Laura: That's what I'm thinking. Anyways, thanks a lot for today. Also, it was nice talking with you. I hope that I haven't interrupted your day too much. I mean, you spent a lot of time (4)[   ] [   ].

Toru: Don't worry. I enjoyed the conversation with you. You know ... maybe we can see (5)[   ] [   ] sometime on campus.

Laura: Oh, definitely. Can I (6)[   ] [   ] contact information?

Toru: Sure.

Laura: All right. I'm going to the station. Where are you going?

Toru: I'm going to study at the library.

Laura: Cool. All right ... let's (7)[   ] [   ] [   ]. Have a good one.

Toru: You too.

Task 　　語句を並べ替えて、<u>留学生など</u>を迎える時に使える表現を英語で書きましょう。

※文頭の語句も、選択肢の中では小文字で記しています。

1. 日本は初めてですか？

   Is [your first time / in Japan / this] ?

α	だれが	する(です)	だれ・なに	どこ	いつ
Is					

注）αは疑問文や接続詞を使った文などで使います。

2. ここで靴を脱いでくださいね。

   Please [your shoes / here / take off].

α	だれが	する（です）	だれ・なに	どこ	いつ
Please					

3. 週に2回、洗濯をしてあげますね。

   [we / twice a week / your clothes / will wash].

だれが	する（です）	だれ・なに	どこ	いつ

4. 何か質問はありますか？

   Do [have / you / any questions] ?

α	だれが	する（です）	だれ・なに	どこ	いつ
Do					

It's Your Turn!

こんな時、あなたならどうする？

慣れない英語を話す際、なかなか単語が出てこないことがあります。そんな時は、自分の表現力を駆使しつつ、相手の協力を得てコミュニケーションをとることも可能です。ここでは、単語当てゲームを通して、言いたい単語が浮かばない時の対処法を練習してみましょう。

Task ▮▮ Explaining & Guessing

Q. ペアになり、出題者と回答者を決めましょう。

［出題者］先生に与えられたお題の中から1つ英単語を選び、<u>その単語自体は使わずに英語で</u>説明しましょう。

［回答者］相手の説明している英単語を推測しましょう。制限時間内に、何問正解できるでしょうか？

例）A さん: **This is a yellow fruit. Monkeys like it.**
　　B さん: **It's a banana, right?**

 Sample Response

必要に応じて会話例を聞くことができます。

Task ▮▮▮ 以下の文章を読んで、設問に答えましょう。

Working Holiday

Do you wish to live and work abroad? If you are young, you could think about getting a working holiday visa. Many countries participate in working holiday programs, and depending on your nationality, you can live and work in one of those countries. The visas usually last for 12 months, and there are some rules and restrictions about what kind of work you can do. In some cases, it is possible to study for a short time, too. Different countries offer different working holiday programs. There are many kinds of possibilities.

The working holiday visa gives young people the chance to travel as well as live and work abroad. Being able to work abroad will not only help cover travel costs, but also give you the chance to experience life in a different language and culture. You will also learn different perspectives and values.

1) According to the passage, what is the purpose of getting a working holiday visa?
   (A) To follow some rules
   (B) To check their nationalities
   (C) To learn what they can do
   (D) To live and work abroad

2) According to the passage, what can young people gain from going on a working holiday?
   (A) Daily habits
   (B) Different perspectives
   (C) Travel plans
   (D) Work-life balance

3) If you had a chance to go on a working holiday, where would you go and what would you do?

   ....

   ....

   ....

   ....

   ....

Unit 4

Commuting by Train

二人の出会いから数日後、ToruはLauraの近況が気になり電話をしてみることにしました。その翌日、Lauraが経験した日本の「文化」とは？

Target 電車の乗換説明に使える英語表現

Watching the Video Clip (1st time)

 Task ▓▓ 動画を見た後、以下の問いに答えましょう。

Q. Which of the following sentences is true?

(A) Laura has forgotten about Toru.

(B) Laura and Toru will meet at 9 A.M.

(C) Many Americans usually drive to school or work.　　　(　　　　)

17)) Words & Expressions

Task ▓▓ イラストを見て、フレーズを完成させましょう。

1.

私のことを覚えていますか？
Do you (r　　　　　) me?

2.

学校まで電車を利用します。
I will (t　　　　　) the train to school.

3.

私は人混みに慣れています。
I am used to the (c　　　　　).

4.

湘南大学まで一緒に歩きませんか？
Can we (w　　　　　) together to Shonan University?

Task ▌▌▌ もう一度動画を見て、以下の問いに答えましょう。

Q1. ストーリーに沿った正しい順番に並べなさい。

(A) Laura and Toru meet each other in front of the train station.

(B) Toru asks Laura if they can go to school together.

(C) Laura sees many people on the train.

(   ) → (   ) → (   )

Q2. Why is Laura surprised?

(A) Because Toru calls Laura

(B) Because many people are on a train

(C) Because Toru wakes up early

(   )

Summary

Task ▌▌▌ 選択肢から適切な単語を選び、Summary を完成させましょう。

Summary of the Dialogue

A few days later, Toru [¹   ] Laura and asks how she is doing, and they [²   ] to meet at the station and walk to school together. The next morning, they meet up in front of the station. Laura is surprised at how [³   ] the train is. Toru says that it is [⁴   ] because he has probably become accustomed to it.

calls	usual	decide	crowded

Dialogue

🔊18 Task ▮▮▮ もう一度動画を見て、以下の空欄に当てはまる語を聞き取りましょう。

🔊19 **Laura:** Hello?

スタジオ音声版 **Toru:** Hello, Laura, (1) [　　　　] [　　　　　] Toru Asano. Do you remember me?

Laura: Of course. Toru, how could I (2) [　　　　] [　　　　]?

Toru: How are you doing?

Laura: Great. My host mother is really nice. She helps me a lot.

Toru: Oh ... good. By the way, you know, tomorrow is the first day of school. Will you go to school (3) [　　　　] [　　　　]?

Laura: Yeah, I will take the train to school.

Toru: Me too. Can we walk together to campus?

Laura: You mean ... from the station? Sure. What time (4) [　　　　] [　　　] meet?

Toru: Well, probably at 8:00 A.M.

Laura: 8:00 is okay with me. See you then.

Laura: Good morning. Toru, how are you today?

Toru: I'm good. And you?

Laura: Just fine. But ... (5) [　　　　] [　　　　] so many people on the train. I was very surprised.

Toru: I know how you feel. But I'm afraid it's usual. I'm probably (6) [　　　　] [　　　　] the crowd.

Laura: Why are there so many people on the train?

Toru: Well ... I don't know. Probably most people go to school or work by train.

Laura: I see. In the United States, we (7) [　　　　] [　　　　] to school or work.

Task ▓▓ 語句を並べ替えて、電車の乗換説明に使える表現を英語で書きましょう。

※文頭の語句も、選択肢の中では小文字で記しています。

1. そこまで案内しますよ。

[there / can take / you / I].

だれが	する（です）	だれ・なに	どこ	いつ

2. まず中央線に乗ってください。

[the Chuo Line / take / first].

だれが	する（です）	だれ・なに	どこ	いつ

3. 渋谷で電車を乗り換える必要があります。

[have to / you / trains / at Shibuya / change].

だれが	する（です）	だれ・なに	どこ	いつ

4. 渋谷に着いたら、そこで駅員さんに尋ねてくださいね。

[to Shibuya / there / the station staff / get / can ask / you].

α	だれが	する（です）	だれ・なに	どこ	いつ
When	you				

注）接続詞を使った文などでは、2段目を使って考えます。

It's Your Turn!

こんな時、あなたならどうする？

海外から日本を訪れた人にとって、電車の乗り方・乗り換えは難しいものです。ここでは、電車の乗り換えの説明を練習しましょう。

Task ▮▮▮ Giving Transfer Information

Q1. あなたは今、平成（Heisei）駅にいます。行きたい駅を決め、そこまでの道のりを説明する英語を考えてみましょう。

Q2. ではパートナーの説明を聞き、どの駅への行き方を説明しているか聞き取ってみましょう。その後、役割を変え、もう一度タスクを行いましょう。

例）Aさん：**You are at Tokyo Station now. Take the Chuo Line first and change trains ...**

Bさん：**It's ... station!**

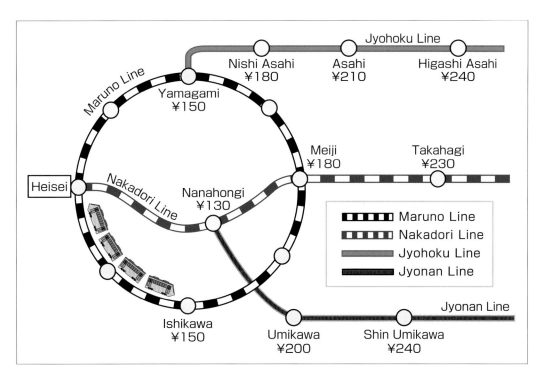

Sample Response

必要に応じて会話例を聞くことができます。

Task ▓ 以下の文章を読んで、設問に答えましょう。

Train Manners

Japan is famous for its efficient transport system. People from abroad are often amazed by not only how efficient the railway networks are but also how clean the trains and stations are. They can be surprised by how polite and helpful the railway staff are, too.

However, unfortunately some passengers on trains are not so polite. They do not offer their seats to passengers with disabilities or elderly passengers. They stay in their own worlds. They listen to loud music or stare at their phone without making eye contact. Some seated passengers even pretend to be asleep! Even then, passengers who don't look Japanese often get stared at, and at times some people refuse to go near them. These kinds of behavior cannot be called "good manners." Just a simple gesture of kindness will improve everyone's journey.

1) According to the passage, what is Japan famous for?
   (A) Good manners
   (B) Passengers
   (C) Transport system
   (D) Railway staff

2) According to the passage, what is an example of showing good manners?
   (A) Offering seats to others
   (B) Listening to loud music
   (C) Pretending to be asleep
   (D) Avoiding eye contact

3) Describe any good/bad manners you have seen in Japan.

Taking Classes

Target 物事の描写に使える英語表現 (1)

キャンパスの掲示板前で、ToruとLauraが新学期の授業について話しています。Lauraにオススメの授業はどのようなものでしょうか？

Watching the Video Clip (1st time)

Task ///// 動画を見た後、以下の問いに答えましょう。

Q. Which of the following sentences is true?

(A) Laura has decided her classes.

(B) Toru is studying about Japanese pop culture.

(C) Everybody in Mr. Nakagawa's class speaks good English.   (   )

22 Words & Expressions

Task ///// イラストを見て、フレーズを完成させましょう。

1.

あまり多くの選択肢がないです。
I don't have many (c   ).

2.

このクラスを履修してみたら？
Why don't you (t   ) this class?

3.

興味深いです！
(S   ) interesting!

4.

それから、決めます。
Then, I will make a (d   ).

Watching the Video Clip (2nd time)

Task ▓▓ もう一度動画を見て、以下の問いに答えましょう。

Q1. ストーリーに沿った正しい順番に並べなさい。

(A) Laura becomes interested in the Japanese pop culture class.

(B) Toru introduces Mr. Nakagawa's class to Laura.

(C) Laura asks Toru about his classes.

(   ) → (   ) → (   )

Q2. What will Laura most likely do before she registers?

(A) Speak with many sophomore friends

(B) Watch Japanese anime and movies

(C) Visit Mr. Nakagawa's class

(   )

Summary

Task ▓▓ 選択肢から適切な単語を選び、Summaryを完成させましょう。

Summary of the Dialogue

Laura and Toru are talking about class registration. He says that he has
[1   ] for two elective classes, and he [2   ] that
she take Mr. Nakagawa's class. He [3   ] her that the class is about
Japanese pop culture and that it is [4   ] in English. She becomes
interested and asks if she can attend before making a decision.

tells	recommends	taught	registered

28

Dialogue

🔊(23))) Task ▮▮▮ もう一度動画を見て、以下の空欄に当てはまる語を聞き取りましょう。

🔊(24)))
スタジオ音声版

Laura: I have to decide (1)[   ] [   ] to take by next Monday. Have you registered for your classes yet?

Toru: Yeah. I (2)[   ] [   ] yesterday. You know, I'm a sophomore, and I don't have a lot of choices.

Laura: Oh … you have a lot of (3)[   ] classes. Are you taking any elective classes?

Toru: Yes, but I have only two electives. I'm taking Mr. Nakagawa's class. Oh... (4)[   ] [   ] [   ] take this class?

Laura: What kind of class is it?

Toru: Well, (5)[   ] [   ] [   ] Japanese pop culture: you know, anime, music, movies … things like that. He does all of his lessons in English. (6)[   ] [   ] [   ] students are international students. The other half are Japanese students, but most of them speak good English.

Laura: Sounds interesting. Can I go to his class first … then, I'll (7)[   ] [   ] [   ]?

Toru: I think that'll be fine.

29

Task ▓▓ 語句を並べ替えて、物事の描写に使える表現を英語で書きましょう。

※文頭の語句も、選択肢の中では小文字で記しています。

1. 2人の男の子が公園でサッカーをしています。

[are playing / in the park / two boys / soccer].

だれが	する（です）	だれ・なに	どこ	いつ

2. 女の子が今、犬の散歩をしています。

[now / is walking / a girl / a dog].

だれが	する（です）	だれ・なに	どこ	いつ

3. 男性がテーブルの上でケーキを切っています。

[a man / on the table / a cake / is cutting].

だれが	する（です）	だれ・なに	どこ	いつ

4. 女性が空き瓶をゴミ箱に捨てています。

[a woman / an empty bottle / into a trash can / is throwing].

だれが	する（です）	だれ・なに	どこ	いつ

It's Your Turn!

こんな時、あなたならどうする？

今回の動画の中でToruが授業内容の説明をしていたように、物事を描写・説明する力は日常会話でも大切です。ここでは、描写力を鍛える練習をしましょう。

Task **Describing a Picture (1)**

Q. Picture 1 から順番に、ペアで交互に以下の絵を描写してみましょう。

[Picture 1]

[Picture 2]

[Picture 3]

[Picture 4]

Sample Response

必要に応じて会話例を聞くことができます。

Read, Think, and Write

 Task 以下の文章を読んで、設問に答えましょう。

Join the Club

While at university, a lot of students not only study for their courses but also join clubs and societies. From sports, theater, and art to politics, there are many kinds of clubs and societies that you can be a part of. Joining a club or society is a great way to enjoy your free time and meet people with similar interests and hobbies. Of course, you can meet students with similar interests in your classes, but when you join a club or society, you get the opportunity to meet people from different courses and colleges. Some students even decide on which university to attend because of the clubs and societies that are on offer. Becoming a member of a club or society while you are a university student can become an important, motivating part of your university life. The things you learn and experience might lead you to new paths.

1) Apart from classes, where can you meet people with similar interests and hobbies?
   (A) Art events
   (B) Theaters
   (C) Different colleges
   (D) Clubs and societies

2) According to the passage, how are clubs and societies different from classes?
   (A) There are people from different courses and colleges.
   (B) It is an important part of university life.
   (C) Activities are more motivating and fun.
   (D) There are students with similar interests.

3) Are you a member of a club or society? If so, what club or society are you in? If not, what kind of club or society would you be interested in?

Unit 6

Talking with a Teacher

Lauraが履修相談をしに中川先生のオフィスを訪ねてきました。会話から先生と学生とのやり取りを学びましょう。

Target 褒める時に使える英語表現

Watching the Video Clip (1st time)

Task 動画を見た後、以下の問いに答えましょう。

Q. Which of the following sentences is true?

(A) Mr. Nakagawa is not in his office.

(B) Mr. Nakagawa knows students like his class.

(C) Laura will be in Mr. Nakagawa's next class.

( )

 27)) ## Words & Expressions

Task イラストを見て、フレーズを完成させましょう。

1.

少しだけ話す時間がありますか？

May I (t) to you for a minute?

2.

お先にどうぞ。

(G) ahead.

3.

聞いて安心しました。

I am glad to (h) that.

4.

勉強頑張ってください。

(G) (l) with your studies.

Task ▨▨▨ もう一度動画を見て、以下の問いに答えましょう。

Q1. ストーリーに沿った正しい順番に並べなさい。

    (A) Mr. Nakagawa accepts Laura's request.

    (B) Laura tells Mr. Nakagawa about her life in Japan.

    (C) Laura stops by Mr. Nakagawa's office.

                  (   ) → (   ) → (   )

Q2. What does Mr. Nakagawa think about his students?

    (A) He thinks all the students enjoyed his last class.

    (B) He thinks most students didn't like the lesson of the day.

    (C) He is not sure if his lessons are interesting for them.

                                    (   )

Summary

Task ▨▨▨ 選択肢から適切な単語を選び、Summaryを完成させましょう。

Summary of the Dialogue

Laura goes to Mr. Nakagawa's office after his class is [1   ]. She tells him that she [2   ] his class really interesting, so she asks if she can take it. He gives her permission and tells her to [3   ] by Monday. He then asks about when she [4   ] to Japan and how things are going for her.

came	register	finished	found

Dialogue

 Task ▨ もう一度動画を見て、以下の空欄に当てはまる語を聞き取りましょう。

スタジオ音声版

Laura: Excuse me. Mr. Nakagawa, (1)[　　　] [　　　] [　　　] to you for a minute?

Mr. Nakagawa: Sure. (2)[　　　] [　　　].

Laura: My name is Laura Mueller. I'm an exchange student from the United States. I (3)[　　　] [　　　] today's lesson.

Mr. Nakagawa: I'm (4)[　　　] [　　　] [　　　] that. I'm always trying to make my lessons interesting. But ... sometimes ... I don't know if students really like them.

Laura: I believe most people liked today's lesson. By the way, can I take this class? I was not in your first lesson, but I'm really interested in the content.

Mr. Nakagawa: No problem. (5)[　　　] [　　　] [　　　] register, though. I think you have to do it by next Monday.

Laura: Will do.

Mr. Nakagawa: By the way, when did you come to Japan?

Laura: Just last week.

Mr. Nakagawa: Oh ... last week? How do you (6)[　　　] [　　　] life in Japan?

Laura: So far, so good. But, there are so many things to learn. Everything is so different.

Mr. Nakagawa: I see. Well, (7)[　　　] [　　　] [　　　] your studying. See you in the next class.

Laura: See you, Mr. Nakagawa.

Task 語句を並べ替えて、褒める時に使える表現を英語で書きましょう。

※文頭の語句も、選択肢の中では小文字で記しています。

1. あなたは聞き上手ですね。

[a good listener / are / you].

だれが	する（です）	だれ・なに	どこ	いつ

2. あなたといるといつも楽しい。

[always enjoy / with you / spending time / I].

だれが	する（です）	だれ・なに	どのよう（に）	どこ	いつ

注）だれ・なに の後には、どのよう（に）が続くこともあります。

3. 昨日、私はあなたの発表に感動した。

[yesterday / was impressed with / I / your presentation].

だれが	する（です）	だれ・なに	どこ	いつ

4. それ似合ってますね。

[on you / looks / it / good].

だれが	する（です）	だれ・なに	どこ	いつ

注）だれ・なに には、形容詞（どんなだ）が入ることもあります。

It's Your Turn!

こんな時、あなたならどうする？

Laura が大学の先生との会話で見せたように、会話において「褒め上手」になることは非常に大切です。ここではその方法を練習してみましょう。

Task ▦ Making a Compliment

Q1. 先生が「ある人」を褒めます。誰のことを褒めているか、推測してみましょう。

1. [   ]
2. [   ]

Q2. ペアになり、一人は「ある人」のことを褒め、もう一人はその「ある人」を推測してみましょう。その後、役割を変えてもう一度タスクを行いましょう。

例）A さん：He is really good at baseball. He made a lot of hits both in Japan and the U.S.

B さん：You're talking about Ichiro, right ?

あなたが褒める有名人：[   ]

Sample Response

必要に応じて会話例を聞くことができます。

Task ▮▮▮ 以下の文章を読んで、設問に答えましょう。

The Importance of Listening

Communication is not just about what you say or the way you speak. You must be able to listen, too. When you speak to somebody, you would like them to listen to you, wouldn't you? This goes the other way around, too. When someone speaks to you, they would want you to listen to them.

Listening is essential to good communication. When you show that you're interested in what other people are saying, they will feel valued and respected. In turn, people will show interest when you speak. So, if you are a good listener, there is a good chance that other people will listen to you, too. The quality of a conversation can be found in how well the listener pays attention to the speaker. Having good listening skills is a vital ingredient to good communication. Good communication is a sign of mutual respect.

1) What is the passage mainly about?
   (A) How to speak in public
   (B) What topics to talk about
   (C) When to speak and when not to speak
   (D) How important listening is

2) According to the passage, what shoud the listener do?
   (A) Make eye contact
   (B) Show interest
   (C) Ask questions
   (D) Avoid falling asleep

3) Write about a conversation you enjoyed. Why did you enjoy it?

Unit 7

Finding Friends

Lauraが留学先での新しい友達作りについて
Toruに相談しています。留学経験のあるToruの
アドバイスとは？

Target 自分の趣味や好みを伝える英語表現

Watching the Video Clip (1st time)

Task ▨ 動画を見た後、以下の問いに答えましょう。

Q. Which of the following sentences is true?

(A) Laura feels a little bit sad.

(B) Laura has many foreign friends in Japan.

(C) Laura can make only sunny-side-up eggs. (   )

 ## Words & Expressions

Task ▨ イラストを見て、フレーズを完成させましょう。

1.

外国で友達を見つけるのは大変です。
It is difficult to (f   ) friends
in a foreign country.

2.

どうやって友達を作ったの？
How did you (m   ) friends?

3.

あなたは何に興味がありますか？
What are you (i   ) in?

4.

わたしは料理が大好きです。
I love (c   ).

Task ▦ もう一度動画を見て、以下の問いに答えましょう。

Q1. ストーリーに沿った正しい順番に並べなさい。

(A) Laura says she wants more friends in Japan.

(B) Toru advises Laura about how to make friends.

(C) Laura tells Toru that she loves cooking.

(   ) → (   ) → (   )

Q2. What will Laura most likely do?

(A) Talk to teachers about a problem

(B) Find people who have the same interests

(C) Cook some food for her friends

(   )

Summary

Task ▦ 選択肢から適切な単語を選び、Summaryを完成させましょう。

Summary of the Dialogue

Toru asks Laura how things are going. She tells him that she has not been able to [1   ] many friends. He says that he [2   ] the same problem in the United States, but after a while, he made many friends. He [3   ] how he found and then became friends with someone who shared his interests. He [4   ] that Laura do the same thing.

make	had	suggests	explains

Dialogue

 Task ▌ もう一度動画を見て、以下の空欄に当てはまる語を聞き取りましょう。

Toru: How's school going?

Laura: Not too badly, but ... not too well.

Toru: Not too well? What's your problem?

Laura: Well, it may not be a big deal ... but ... you know, (1)[   ] [   ] [   ] my schoolwork, but ... I haven't made so many friends.

Toru: I see. It's a bit difficult to (2)[   ] [   ] in a foreign country. I had the same problem in the United States.

Laura: Oh, did you? So, did you find some friends (3)[   ] [   ] [   ]?

Toru: Actually, I did.

Laura: That's good to hear. How did you (4)[   ] [   ], can I ask?

Toru: Well, it went like this: I saw a guy with the same interests. And then, he let me into his group. After that, I (5)[   ] [   ] [   ] make more friends.

Laura: That's nice. Maybe I can do the same thing ... find somebody with the same interests.

Toru: Yeah. What are you (6)[   ] [   ], by the way?

Laura: Oh, you didn't know? I (7)[   ] [   ]. Cooking is my life!

Toru: Seriously? I thought you could make only sunny-side-up eggs.

Laura: Toru, sometimes, you're really mean.

Task ▮▮ 語句を並べ替えて、自分の趣味や好みを伝える時に使える表現を英語で書きましょう。

※文頭の語句も、選択肢の中では小文字で記しています。

1. 私の趣味は歌を歌うことです。

[my hobby / singing songs / is].

だれが	する（です）	だれ・なに	どこ	いつ

2. この大学でラグビー部に所属しています。

[belong to / at this university / I / the rugby team].

だれが	する（です）	だれ・なに	どこ	いつ

3. 普段、週に3回はカフェに行きます。

[to a café / usually go / three times a week / I].

だれが	する（です）	だれ・なに	どこ	いつ

4. 漫画のない生活など想像できません。

[I / life without *manga* / cannot imagine].

だれが	する（です）	だれ・なに	どこ	いつ

It's Your Turn!

こんな時、あなたならどうする？

友人を見つける良い方法の一つは、共通の趣味や好みをもつ相手を見つけることです。ここでは、自分の趣味や好みを伝える練習をしてみましょう。

Task ▓▓▓ Talking About Your Favorite Things

Q. ペアになり、speakerとlistenerを決めましょう。

[speaker] あなたの趣味や好みについて、<u>1分間</u>、英語で話し続けましょう。

[listener] メモを取らずにspeakerの話を聞いた後、覚えていることを可能な限り、英語で再現してみましょう。

例）Aさん：I love playing the clarinet in the wind orchestra. I practice it three times a week....

　　Bさん：You like playing the clarinet in the wind orchestra very much. You play it three times a week....

あなたの趣味や好み　[　　　　　　　　　　　　　　　　　　　　　　　　　]

 Sample Response

必要に応じて会話例を聞くことができます。

Task ▮▮▮ 以下の文章を読んで、設問に答えましょう。

Getting to Know Yourself

Meeting different people is important, but it is also important to get to know yourself. Make sure you create time for yourself everyday. By spending time alone, you will discover many things about yourself and the world. You will get the chance to think and dream without any distractions. Spending time on your own is an opportunity to set yourself free. You could even take yourself out on a date, and treat yourself to your favorite meal! Of course, it can be difficult to make time for yourself when you are busy. But you could spend a few minutes before going to bed to look back on your day. You could keep a diary or journal, too. When you make time for yourself, you will make new discoveries, and learn more about what you really want to do in life.

1) What can you discover by spending time alone?
   (A) Things about yourself and the world
   (B) Somebody to go on a date with
   (C) Different kinds of people
   (D) A lot of free time

2) According to the passage, what can you do to get to know yourself when you are busy?
   (A) Go to bed early
   (B) Eat your favorite meal
   (C) Keep a diary
   (D) Think and dream

3) What do you usually do when you are by yourself?

   ----

8 Potluck

Toru が落ち込んでいる Laura のために面白い
パーティーを思いついたようです。Toru の考える
パーティーとは？

Target パーティーなどの集まりで使える英語表現

Watching the Video Clip (1st time)

Task 動画を見た後、以下の問いに答えましょう。

Q. Which of the following sentences is true?

    (A) Laura cooks everything with Toru.

    (B) Lasagna is not Toru's favorite food.

    (C) Laura meets many friends at the party. ( )

37)) Words & Expressions

Task イラストを見て、フレーズを完成させましょう。

1.

いい考えがある！

I've (g) an idea!

2.

それは素晴らしい案ですね！

That's an (a) idea!

3.

将来のことをまだ決めていません。

I haven't (d) my future
yet.

4.

とても楽しかったです。

I (h) a lot of fun.

Task 〓 もう一度動画を見て、以下の問いに答えましょう。

Q1. ストーリーに沿った正しい順番に並べなさい。

(A) Laura says she can cook lasagna.

(B) Laura and Toru decide to hold a party.

(C) Many friends come to the party.

(   ) → (   ) → (   )

Q2. What does Laura think about the party?

(A) It is very short.

(B) It is very tiring.

(C) It is successful.

(   )

Summary

Task 〓 選択肢から適切な単語を選び、Summary を完成させましょう。

Summary of the Dialogue

Toru gets an idea for how to help Laura make friends. Because she likes to cook, he suggests [1   ] an international potluck party. He says he will [2   ] some of his friends. When Laura tells him that she will probably [3   ] lasagna, he says it is his favorite dish. The party is a [4   ]. The people and the food are great, and Laura makes some new friends.

success	cook	invite	holding

Dialogue

 Task ▓▓ もう一度動画を見て、以下の空欄に当てはまる語を聞き取りましょう。

Toru: I've got (1)[　　　　　] [　　　　　]!

Laura: What is it?

Toru: Let's hold an international potluck party. Everybody can bring their local food. We can have fun over a variety of foods. How does that sound?

Laura: Oh Toru, that's an amazing idea! You're sometimes (2)[　　　　　] [　　　　　]!

Toru: I think I'm always smart. Anyway, some of my friends really like cooking. I can (3)[　　　　　] [　　　　　]. You know Midori and Saori, right?

Laura: Yeah, they're good cooks. I wonder what they would make: rice balls?

Toru: No. They (4)[　　　　　] [　　　　　] [　　　　　] *chirashi-zushi*—a kind of *sushi*—vinegar flavored rice with some vegetables or seafood.

Laura: Sounds yummy...

Toru: It is. By the way, what are you going to make?

Laura: Well, I (5)[　　　　　] [　　　　　] yet. But ... lasagna would be nice.

Toru: Lasagna? Can you make it?

Laura: Yes, I can. Why are you so suspicious?

Toru: No ... lasagna is (6)[　　　　　] [　　　　　] [　　　　　]. If you made it, that'd be great.

Toru: (7)[　　　　　] [　　　　　] [　　　　　] the party?

Laura: Yes, I had a lot of fun. The food was great. And I was able to meet so many nice people. Thanks, Toru.

Task ▦ 語句を並べ替えて、パーティーなどの集まりで使える表現を英語で書きましょう。

※文頭の語句も、選択肢の中では小文字で記しています。

1. ご出身はどちらですか？
   Where do [from / come / you]?

α	だれが	する（です）	だれ・なに	どこ	いつ
Where do					

2. あなたたちはお互い知り合いですか？
   Do [know / you guys / each other]?

α	だれが	する（です）	だれ・なに	どこ	いつ
Do					

3. それは初めて知りました！
   [have never heard / before / that / I]!

だれが	する（です）	だれ・なに	どこ	いつ

4. 暇な時に何をしてますか？
   What do [in your free time / do / you]?

α	だれが	する（です）	だれ・なに	どこ	いつ
What do					

It's Your Turn!

こんな時、あなたならどうする？

海外の人はパーティー好きだと言われます。もしあなたがパーティーに招かれたら、どんな会話をして相手との交流を深めますか？ここでは、そのような場面でのコミュニケーションを練習しましょう。

Task ▮▮ Party Talk

Q1. 初対面の相手に尋ねたい質問を三つ考えてみましょう。すべて英語で表現できますか？

- _____
- _____
- _____

Q2. あなたは今、Ken主催のパーティーに参加しています。三人程度のグループになり、相手とは初対面のつもりで、Q1.で考えた質問をできるだけ自然な流れで尋ね合ってみましょう。グループで3分間、会話を続けることができますか？

Sample Response

必要に応じて会話例を聞くことができます。

Read, Think, and Write

41))) Task ▉ 以下の文章を読んで、設問に答えましょう。

Celebrating with Food

  We all need to eat to live. But food is not just for survival. Food is something to enjoy and is used for celebrating, too. All over the world, people eat special kinds of food on special occasions. Food can be symbolic and have different meanings. Let's take a look at what people eat on New Year's Day. In Spain, the tradition is to eat twelve grapes. The grapes represent the twelve months of the year and are symbols of good luck. Traditionally in Turkey, people smash pomegranates on their doorsteps. The pomegranate seeds scatter all over the floor and look like beautiful jewels. The seeds are symbols of good fortune. People in Nigeria eat lentils. Lentils are shaped like coins and are symbols of prosperity. Interestingly, in Italy people eat lentils in the new year for good fortune too, because the lentils also represent money. Throughout the year, the meals we eat can have different meanings. With these different meanings and flavors, we can create some wonderful memories with food.

1) According to the passage, what do people do on special occasions?
 (A) Celebrate the new year
 (B) Wish for good luck
 (C) Have wonderful memories
 (D) Eat special kinds of food

2) In Turkey, what do pomegranates symbolize?
 (A) Beautiful jewels
 (B) Good fortune
 (C) Twelve months of the year
 (D) Coins

3) What do you like to eat on New Year's Day?

Unit 9 *Sumo*

相撲に興味があるLauraは何やらToruに相談を
しています。Lauraはどのような方法で相撲を見
に行くか二人の会話から学びましょう。

 Target 物事の描写に使える英語表現 (2)

Watching the Video Clip (1ˢᵗ time)

Task 動画を見た後、以下の問いに答えましょう。

Q. Which of the following sentences is true?

(A) Laura doesn't like sports.

(B) Toru is going to buy one ticket.

(C) Laura knows that *sumo* tickets are very expensive. (   )

Disc 2
 1))) Words & Expressions

Task イラストを見て、フレーズを完成させましょう。

1.

両国で相撲が観たいです。
I would like to (s   ) *sumo* in Ryogoku.

2.

チケットを注文してくれませんか？
Can you (o   ) tickets?

3.

私が相撲のチケットを予約します。
I'll (r   ) *sumo* tickets.

4.

その値段なら大丈夫です。
That (p   ) is okay.

51

Task ░░░ もう一度動画を見て、以下の問いに答えましょう。

Q1. ストーリーに沿った正しい順番に並べなさい。

    (A) Laura asks Toru to order her a *sumo* ticket.

    (B) Toru promises to reserve a *sumo* ticket for Laura.

    (C) Laura and Toru decide to go to see *sumo* together.

                              (   ) → (   ) → (   )

Q2. What will Toru probably do next Wednesday?

    (A) He will reserve *sumo* tickets.

    (B) He will watch *sumo*.

    (C) He will call to order the *sumo* tickets.

                                                       (   )

Summary

Task ░░░ 選択肢から適切な単語を選び、Summary を完成させましょう。

Summary of the Dialogue

Laura asks Toru to [¹   ] her a *sumo* ticket. At first, he is [²   ] because she told him that she does not like sports. However, she says that *sumo* is [³   ], and she wants to see it at least once. Toru suggests going together. Laura is surprised to hear how [⁴   ] the tickets are, but she agrees on the price.

          get   unique   expensive   surprised

Dialogue

3)))
スタジオ音声版

Laura: Toru, could you (1) [   ] [   ] [   ]?

Toru: Sure. What's wrong?

Laura: I'd like to go see *sumo*, but ... I don't know (2) [   ] [   ] [   ] a ticket. Could you order one for me?

Toru: Oh, I didn't know you were interested in *sumo*. You told me you didn't like sports.

Laura: Right. But, you know, *sumo* is very unique. (3) [   ] [   ] [   ] most Americans think they want to see *sumo* at least once.

Toru: I see. *Sumo* has a long history. So, probably it's a good idea to watch it while you're in Japan. I can (4) [   ] [   ]. When do you want to see *sumo*?

Laura: Well, Wednesday or Friday, next week would be best.

Toru: Wednesday or Friday ... Laura, (5) [   ] [   ] on Wednesday. Would it be okay if I joined you?

Laura: Sure. I was thinking of going alone, but you're welcome to come with me.

Toru: OK. After I get tickets, I'll call you. By the way, one *sumo* ticket costs about ten thousand yen. Is that (6) [   ] [   ] [   ]?

Laura: Oh ... is it that expensive? I can't believe it. Well ... I guess I can (7) [   ] [   ] [   ]. I hope we'll really have a good time. Anyways, thanks.

Task 　語句を並べ替えて、物事の描写に使える表現を英語で書きましょう。

※文頭の語句も、選択肢の中では小文字で記しています。

1. 写真の右側に女性が三人います。

   There are [three women / of the picture / on the right side].

だれが	する（です）	だれ・なに	どこ	いつ
There	are			

2. 絵の真ん中に青いカップが二つ見えます。

   [can see / in the center / I / of the picture / two blue cups].

だれが	する（です）	だれ・なに	どこ	いつ

3. 背景には山が見えますよ。

   [mountains / can see / I / in the background].

だれが	する（です）	だれ・なに	どこ	いつ

4. 手前にはウサギのようなものがいます。

   [there / in the foreground / is / something like a rabbit].

だれが	する（です）	だれ・なに	どこ	いつ

It's Your Turn!

こんな時、あなたならどうする？

Unit 5で述べたように、物事を描写・説明する力は重要です。ここでは「絵復元タスク」を用いて、楽しみながらスピーキング力を鍛えましょう。

Task ▓▓ Describing a Picture (2)

Q1. 先生がある絵の説明をします。その説明を元に、絵を復元してみましょう。

[Picture 1]

[Picture 2]

Q2. 先生が、あなたとパートナーにそれぞれ異なる絵を配ります。一人は絵の説明をし、もう一人はその説明を元に絵を復元してみましょう。その後、役割を変えてもう一度タスクを行いましょう。

[復元したパートナーの絵]

🔊4 **Sample Response**

必要に応じて会話例を聞くことができます。

Read, Think, and Write

 Task ▥ 以下の文章を読んで、設問に答えましょう。

Traditional Wrestling in Mongolia and Japan

There is a long history of wrestling in both Mongolia and Japan. Mongolian wrestling is called *bökh*. Japanese wrestling is called *sumo*. Both are traditional and very popular today, too. Originally, *bökh* was a sport to train warriors and make them strong. There are ancient cave paintings in Mongolia from 7000 B.C. that show two people wrestling each other, surrounded by crowds of people. In Japan there are prehistoric wall paintings which show people dancing in a field. Many believe that sumo originates from this dance ritual which was performed to pray for a good harvest.

These days, *bökh* and *sumo* are enjoyed as entertainment. *Bökh* is the most popular national sport in Mongolia, and wrestling festivals are held every summer. In Japan, there are six professional *sumo* tournaments a year. People of all ages, young and old, love traditional wrestling in Mongolia and Japan.

1) What is popular in Mongolia and Japan?
   (A) Prehistoric cave paintings
   (B) Historical sports
   (C) Traditional wrestling
   D. Sports festivals

2) When are wrestling festivals held in Mongolia?
   (A) All ages
   (B) Six times a year
   (C) 7000 B.C.
   (D) Every summer

3) What kind of sports do you like? Why? If you don't like any sports, why not?

Four Seasons

皆さんは四季の中でどの季節がいちばん好きですか？ LauraとToruの季節への考え方の違いを学びましょう。

Target 好きな季節の説明に使える英語表現

Watching the Video Clip (1ˢᵗ time)

Task 動画を見た後、以下の問いに答えましょう。

Q. Which of the following sentences is true?

(A) Laura has seen cherry blossoms in the United States.

(B) Toru enjoys hot weather in summer.

(C) Laura wants to see colorful autumn leaves in Japan.　　　(　　　)

🔊 Words & Expressions

Task イラストを見て、フレーズを完成させましょう。

1.

その美しい景色に感動しました。

We were so (i　　　　　　) by the beautiful scenery.

2.

私たちは湘南大学を卒業します。

We are going to (g　　　　　) from Shonan University.

3.

雨のせいで明日は桜を見に行けない。

We can't go see the (c　　　　　) blossomes tomorrow because of rain.

4.

私のお気に入りの季節は冬です。

My (f　　　　　) season is winter.

Task ◼◼◼ もう一度動画を見て、以下の問いに答えましょう。

Q1. ストーリーに沿った正しい順番に並べなさい。

(A) Laura is very impressed when she sees the cherry blossoms for the first time.

(B) Laura and Toru go to see the cherry blossoms.

(C) Laura and Toru discuss the differences between the seasons in Japan and in the United States.

(   ) → (   ) → (   )

Q2. Why does Laura like the summer season?

(A) Because she doesn't have school

(B) Because she doesn't like dry weather

(C) Because winter in her hometown is freezing

(   )

Summary

Task ◼◼◼ 選択肢から適切な単語を選び、Summary を完成させましょう。

Summary of the Dialogue

Laura goes to Kyoto with Toru and sees the cherry blossoms for the first time. She thinks they are lovely. She and Toru then [1   ] the differences between the seasons in Japan and in the United States. They also talk about which seasons they like and don't like. Toru does not like the [2   ] and humid Japanese summers, but Laura loves the [3   ] summers of her hometown. Toru is looking forward to the [4   ] colors of fall, while Laura says that winters in her hometown are freezing.

hot	dry	beautiful	discuss

Dialogue

7))) **Task** ▮▮▮ もう一度動画を見て、以下の空欄に当てはまる語を聞き取りましょう。

8)))
スタジオ音声版

Laura: Wow, it's so lovely.

Toru: I'm glad you like it. (1) [   ] [   ] [   ] cherry blossoms in the United States?

Laura: No, actually it's my first time. I'm (2) [   ] [   ] by this beautiful scenery. No wonder most Japanese people have special feelings toward cherry blossoms.

Toru: Also, you can see cherry blossoms for only a limited time. (3) [   ] [   ] [   ] or enroll in school this season. This also makes them special.

Laura: I see. People have picnics under the trees, right?

Toru: Yeah, it is called *Hanami*. By the way, are there four seasons in the United States?

Laura: Ah ..., kind of. (4) [   ] [   ] [   ], we have all four seasons, but in a place like ... Hawaii, it's warm throughout the year. And ... in Alaska, it's cold all year.

Toru: I see. What is your favorite season?

Laura: I like summer. You know, I don't have school, and the days are longer.

Toru: I don't like summer. It is very (5) [   ] [   ] [   ].

Laura: I see. In my hometown, it's not so humid. It's (6) [   ] [   ].

Toru: Interesting. How about winter? Is it very cold?

Laura: Yes, (7) [   ] [   ] [   ]. You can't walk outside unless you have a very heavy coat. I don't like winter much. Which season do you like best?

Toru: I like fall best. You can see colorful leaves—yellow, red, and brown—and they are very beautiful.

Laura: Oh, I want to see that.

Task ▐▐▐ 語句を並べ替えて、好きな季節の説明に使える表現を英語で書きましょう。

※文頭の語句も、選択肢の中では小文字で記しています。

1. 春が一番好きです。

[spring / best / I / like].

だれが	する（です）	だれ・なに	どのよう（に）	どこ	いつ

2. 夏には多くの人が花火大会に行きます。

[go / in summer / a lot of people / to fireworks festivals].

だれが	する（です）	だれ・なに	どこ	いつ

3. 秋には紅葉がありますね。

[turn / in fall / leaves / red and yellow].

だれが	する（です）	だれ・なに	どこ	いつ

注）だれ・なに には、形容詞（どんなだ）が入ることもあります。

4. 冬には友達とスキーを楽しむことができます。

[with friends of mine / can enjoy / in winter / I / skiing].

だれが	する（です）	だれ・なに	どのよう（に）	どこ	いつ

It's Your Turn!

こんな時、あなたならどうする？

季節や天気の話は、万国共通の便利な話題です。ここでは、自分の好きな季節を理由をつけて話す練習をしましょう。

Task ▊▊ Talking About Seasons

Q. ペアになり、speaker と listener を決めましょう。

[speaker] あなたの好きな季節と嫌いな季節について、<u>1分間</u>、英語で話し続けましょう。

[listener] <u>メモを取らずに</u> speaker の話を聞いた後、覚えていることを可能な限り英語で再現しましょう。

例）Aさん：I like summer best. In summer, I can swim in the sea....

Bさん：You like summer best because you can swim in the sea....

あなたの一番好きな季節　[　　　　　　　　　　]
あなたの一番嫌いな季節　[　　　　　　　　　　]

 9))

Sample Response

必要に応じて会話例を聞くことができます。

Read, Think, and Write

 Task 以下の文章を読んで、設問に答えましょう。

Climate Change

Climate change is affecting the whole world, from the oceans and forests to farms and cities. Venice, Italy gets a lot of floods now because of rising sea levels. In the Swiss Alps, there is less snowfall in the winter, and glaciers are melting in the Arctic and Antartica. The Amazon, which is the largest rainforest on Earth, has been getting droughts and wildfires. From floods in Venice to droughts in the Amazon, climate change is making the earth's environment more and more unstable. The seasons are affected, too. You might enjoy a lovely sunny spring's day one day and on the next day have heavy snowfall. In recent years, the summer season in Japan has been getting longer and even hotter. On the other hand, spring, autumn, and winter are getting shorter and warmer. Scientists warn that climate change will continue to get worse. The world now faces not only climate "change" but also a climate "emergency."

1) Why is Venice getting a lot of floods?
   (A) Because the seasons are affected
   (B) Because snow is falling heavily
   (C) Because the summer is hotter
   (D) Because sea levels are rising

2) According to the passage, what are scientists saying about climate change?
   (A) Climate change will get worse.
   (B) Glaciers are melting.
   (C) The weather is unstable.
   (D) There will be more droughts.

3) Write about one thing you can do to reduce pollution.

Green Tea

皆さんは緑茶 (green tea) をよく飲みますか？ ア
メリカ人のLauraは緑茶に対してどう感じるので
しょうか？

Target 物事の描写に使える英語表現（3）

Watching the Video Clip (1st time)

Task ▊▊▊ 動画を見た後、以下の問いに答えましょう。

Q. Which of the following sentences is true?

(A) Laura has never drunk green tea in the United States.

(B) Laura enjoys the flavor of green tea.

(C) The green tea is more bitter than Laura expected. (   )

11))) Words & Expressions

Task ▊▊▊ イラストを見て、フレーズを完成させましょう。

1.

一緒にレストランに行きませんか？
(W   ) don't we go to a
restaurant together?

2.

このお茶にしてみましょう！
Let's (t   ) this tea!

3.

四つのレストランのうちの一つに行きましょう！
Let's go to (o   ) of the
(f   ) restaurants!

4.

薬のような味がします。
It (t   ) like medicine.

Task ░░ もう一度動画を見て、以下の問いに答えましょう。

Q1. ストーリーに沿った正しい順番に並べなさい。

(A) Toru is surprised because Laura wants to go to a tea restaurant.

(B) Green tea is too bitter for Laura.

(C) Laura and Toru go to a green tea restaurant.

(　　　　　) → (　　　　　) → (　　　　　)

Q2. What does Toru think about American people?

(A) They always drink green tea.

(B) They put honey in their coffee.

(C) They drink coffee more often than green tea.

(　　　　　)

Summary

Task ░░ 選択肢から適切な単語を選び、Summaryを完成させましょう。

Summary of the Dialogue

Laura and Toru are thirsty, and Laura [1　　　　　　　　　] going to a tea house that serves green tea. She tells him that she has had sweet green tea in the United States. Toru is surprised and says Japanese people do not [2　　　　　　　　　] honey or lemon in their green tea. When Laura [3　　　　　　　　　] the green tea at the restaurant, she [4　　　　　　　　] it really bitter and says, "It tastes like medicine."

put	finds	tries	suggests

Dialogue

 Task ▐ もう一度動画を見て、以下の空欄に当てはまる語を聞き取りましょう。

Toru: Would you like something to drink?

Laura: Sure. (1) [   ] [   ] [   ] go to a tea house— I mean, a green tea place?

Toru: Oh, I thought Americans like coffee (2) [   ] [   ] green tea.

Laura: We do, but it's a rare opportunity (3) [   ] [   ] [   ] something Japanese.

Toru: Have you ever drunk green tea in the United States?

Laura: Yes, only a couple of times.

Toru: (4) [   ] [   ] [   ] like it?

Laura: I kind of liked it. It tasted a bit too sweet.

Toru: Sweet? Green tea is a bitter drink. Probably you drank American green tea, not a Japanese one. We (5) [   ] [   ] any honey or lemon in green tea.

Laura: Oh, I see. Then, I want to drink real green tea.

Toru: Okay. Anyway, there are a lot of green tea houses here. Let's (6) [   ] [   ] [   ] of them.

Laura: Eew ... This is so bitter. (7) [   ] [   ] [   ] medicine. Why do Japanese people drink this?

Toru: You're right. Actually, hundreds of years ago, green tea was medicine. Some people enjoy it because it's healthy.

Laura: Oh, I see.

Task ▓▓ 語句を並べ替えて、物事の描写に使える表現を英語で書きましょう。

※文頭の語句も、選択肢の中では小文字で記しています。

1. 店員さんがレジでお金を数えています。

[is counting / a store clerk / at the register / money].

だれが	する（です）	だれ・なに	どこ	いつ

2. 女の子が右手に財布を持っています。

[a girl / in her right hand / a wallet / is holding].

だれが	する（です）	だれ・なに	どこ	いつ

3. 右にいる男性はだんごを食べていますか？

Is [eating / Japanese sweet dumplings / the man on the right]?

α	だれが	する（です）	だれ・なに	どこ	いつ
Is					

4. 右下の角には何が見えますか？

What can [in the bottom right corner / see / you]?

α	だれが	する（です）	だれ・なに	どこ	いつ
What can					

It's Your Turn!

こんな時、あなたならどうする？

Unit 5, 9で述べたように、物事を描写・説明する力は重要です。ここでは「間違い探しタスク」を通して、楽しみながらスピーキング力を鍛えましょう。

Task　Spot the Differences

Q1. ペアで別の絵を見て、お互いの絵を見ずに口頭で絵描写・質問をする中で、五つの「間違い」を見つけましょう。No gestures & English only!

例）Aさん：**Can you see a woman on the left of the picture?**
　　Bさん：**Yes. She is wearing pants, right?**
　　Aさん：**Really? She is wearing a skirt in my picture!**
　　Bさん：**Oh, then this must be a difference!**
（同様に、残り四つの「間違い」を見つけてみましょう。）

Aさんの絵

Bさんの絵

Q2. 先生が、あなたとパートナーにそれぞれ異なる絵を配ります。
　　Q1と同様に、お互いの絵を見ずに、五つの「間違い」を見つけましょう。

Sample Response

必要に応じて会話例を聞くことができます。

Task 以下の文章を読んで、設問に答えましょう。

History of Tea in Japan

Japan has a long history of tea-drinking. Tea was first introduced to Japan as early as the 8th century, when Japanese priests went to China to learn about its culture. After their trip to China, the priests brought back tea to Japan. In the beginning, tea was used as a kind of medicine. At the time, it was only available to priests and people of noble classes. The roots of Japanese tea culture were set a few hundred years later.

In the 12th century, the monk Eisai went on a pilgrimage to China and brought back tea seeds. These seeds were planted in parts of Kyushu and Kyoto. In Japan, tea leaves were processed in different ways from China. Japanese green tea was born from this process. Over time, green tea became available to the general public and turned into an important part of Japan's culture. Today, people all over the world enjoy drinking green tea.

1) When was Japan first introduced to tea?
   (A) The 12th century
   (B) A long history
   (C) A few hundred years later
   (D) The 8th century

2) What happened in Kyushu and Kyoto in the 12th century?
   (A) Tea seeds were planted.
   (B) Green tea became popular.
   (C) Tea was made into medicine.
   (D) People all over the world drank tea.

3) What is your favorite type of beverage? Why do you like it?

   ....
   ....
   ....
   ....
   ....
   ....

Unit 12 Japanese Food

外国人の友達に日本食を勧めるとしたら何が良いのでしょうか？ 高級な料理はちょっと勧めにくいですよね？ Toru は何を選ぶのでしょうか？

Target 料理の説明に使える英語表現

Watching the Video Clip (1st time)

Task ▓▓▓ 動画を見た後、以下の問いに答えましょう。

Q. Which of the following sentences is true?

(A) Laura wants to have Japanese food.

(B) Only Toru is tired and hungry.

(C) Laura and Toru eat *soba* at the school cafeteria.
( )

16)) Words & Expressions

Task ▓▓▓ イラストを見て、フレーズを完成させましょう。

1.

何が食べたいですか？
What do you want to (e)?

2.

私はうどんにしてみます。
I will (t) *udon*.

3.

塩と胡椒をとってくれませんか？
Could you (p) me the salt and pepper?

4.

お腹いっぱいで、もう食べられません。
I can't eat anymore because I am so (f).

Task ▓▓ もう一度動画を見て、以下の問いに答えましょう。

Q1. ストーリーに沿った正しい順番に並べなさい。

(A) Toru recommends *soba*.

(B) Laura and Toru discuss what they would like to eat.

(C) Laura and Toru go to a *soba* restaurant.

(   ) → (   ) → (   )

Q2. What is the main reason for Laura and Toru to go to the soba restaurant?

(A) Because Laura has never tried real *soba*

(B) Because it is not expensive

(C) Because Toru works at a *soba* restaurant

(   )

Summary

Task ▓▓ 選択肢から適切な単語を選び、Summary を完成させましょう。

Summary of the Dialogue

One day, Laura and Toru are out in Tokyo and are tired and hungry. Laura wants to eat some good Japanese food, so Toru suggests [1   ] *soba*. She says that the *soba* at the school cafeteria is just okay, and Toru [2   ] eating real *soba* at a *soba* restaurant. Laura is pleasantly surprised and says it is [3   ] because of the [4   ] of the soup and the noodles.

delicious	quality	having	recommends

Dialogue

 Task ▦ もう一度動画を見て、以下の空欄に当てはまる語を聞き取りましょう。

Laura: I (1) [   ] [   ] [   ] [   ].

Toru: I'm tired too. Also, I'm hungry.

Laura: Me too. Let's find a place to eat.

Toru: Sounds like a good idea. (2) [   ] [   ] [   ] [   ] [   ] eat — Chinese, Italian, French, or American?

Laura: What!? No way! We are in Tokyo. I'm pretty sure there are a lot of good Japanese restaurants.

Toru: Okay. So ..., what kind of Japanese food do you want to eat? *Sushi*? *Tempura*?

Laura: Well ..., those are (3) [   ] [   ], but you can eat them in the States as well. On top of that, they are a bit pricey.

Toru: They are. How about *soba*? *Soba* is ...

Laura: I know. *Soba* is Japanese-style noodles, right? Actually, I've eaten *soba* at the school cafeteria (4) [   ] [   ] [   ] times, but ... honestly, I'd say it was just okay.

Toru: Oh, Laura. *Soba* at the school cafeteria is just fast food, but you can eat real *soba* at a *soba* restaurant.

Laura: Oh, really? That's good to hear. Then, (5) [   ] [   ] *soba*. Do you know any good *soba* restaurant?

Toru: I researched it yesterday. The one over there is likely to be quite good. Should we go there?

Laura: Why not?

Toru: Do you like it?

Laura: Yeah, the quality of soup and noodles is so different from the *soba* at the cafeteria.

Toru: (6) [   ] [   ] [   ].

Task ▨▨▨ 語句を並べ替えて、料理の説明に使える表現を英語で書きましょう。

※文頭の語句も、選択肢の中では小文字で記しています。

1. 寿司はわさびと醤油につけて食べます。

[sushi / with *wasabi* and soy sauce / eat / we].

だれが	する（です）	だれ・なに	どのよう（に）	どこ	いつ

2. お好み焼きは小麦粉、卵、キャベツなどの様々な材料からできています。

[okonomiyaki / various ingredients / is made from / flour, eggs, and cabbage / such as].

だれが	する（です）	だれ・なに	どこ	いつ

3. おでんは普通、冬に食べます。

[oden / in winter / we / usually have].

だれが	する（です）	だれ・なに	どこ	いつ

4. おせちは新年にいただく伝統的な食事です。

Osechi is [we / during the New Year period / a traditional meal / have].

だれが	する（です）	だれ・なに	どこ	いつ
Osechi	is			

It's Your Turn!

こんな時、あなたならどうする？

「和食」はユネスコ無形文化遺産に登録されています。海外から日本を訪れた方に食文化について質問された時、あなたはその素晴らしさを伝えることができますか？ ここでは、日本の食文化の説明について練習をしましょう。

Task ▌▌ Explaining Food Culture

Q1. 先生が「ある料理」の説明をします。何の料理の説明をしているか、推測してみましょう。

1. [   ]
2. [   ]

Q2. ペアになり、一人は「ある料理」を説明し、もう一人はその「ある料理」を推測してみましょう。その後、役割を変えてもう一度タスクを行いましょう。

あなたが説明する料理： [   ]

19)) **Sample Response**

必要に応じて会話例を聞くことができます。

Task ▍▍▍ 以下の文章を読んで、設問に答えましょう。

Fermented Food

Food has been fermented for thousands of years. From pickles and bread to cheese and chocolate, people all around the world eat fermented food everyday. When food is fermented, it can be preserved. Some fermented foods can be preserved for a long time. People have fermented food to preserve it for thousands of years. There are many different kinds of fermented food, including pickles, bread, cheese, and chocolate, and many ways to ferment food. In Korea, for example, many people ferment different kinds of vegetables and seafood to make their own *kimchi*. In India, milk is fermented to make homemade yogurt called *curd*. Fermented food is not only delicious but also good for your body. Medical and scientific research has shown that fermented food can help people improve their health. Now, fermenting and preserving your own food has become popular. There are many workshops and books that teach how to ferment different kinds of food.

1) When did humans start fermenting food?
   (A) Fairly recently
   (B) Before World War II
   (C) Thousands of years ago
   (D) About three hundred years ago

2) According to the passage, what fermented food is made from milk in India?
   (A) Chocolate
   (B) Cheese
   (C) Yogurt
   (D) Pickles

3) What kind of fermented food do you eat the most? When do you eat it?

Unit 13 Part-Time Jobs

アルバイト先で外国人のお客さんに英語で接客するとき、「いらっしゃいませ」「X円になります」などは何と言うのでしょうか？

🎯 Target アルバイト先で使える英語表現

Watching the Video Clip (1st time)

Task 動画を見た後、以下の問いに答えましょう。

Q. Which of the following sentences is true?

(A) The store is usually not busy because it is in the business district.

(B) Laura buys two different kinds of donuts and a cup of coffee.

(C) Laura will text Toru tomorrow morning. ( )

🔊 21 Words & Expressions

Task イラストを見て、フレーズを完成させましょう。

1.

沢山のお客さんが列に並んで待っています。
Many customers are (w) in line.

2.

おつりをどうぞ。
Here is your (c).

3.

どのようなアルバイトがしたいですか？
(W) (k) of part-time job would you like to have?

4.

私は週末に食料品店で6時間働きます。
I (w) for 6 hours on weekends at a grocery store.

75

Task ▮▮▮ もう一度動画を見て、以下の問いに答えましょう。

Q1. ストーリーに沿った正しい順番に並べなさい。

    (A)   Laura and Toru promise to see each other.

    (B)   Laura buys breakfast.

    (C)   Toru is surprised to see Laura at the store.

(　　　　　) → (　　　　　) → (　　　　　)

Q2. Why does Toru say, "Two donuts?"

    (A)   Because Laura doesn't like donuts

    (B)   Because Toru is joking

    (C)   Because Laura is very hungry   (　　　　　)

Summary

Task ▮▮▮ 選択肢から適切な単語を選び、Summaryを完成させましょう。

Summary of the Dialogue

One day, Laura [1　　　　　　　　] a convenience store to see Toru working. She [2　　　　　　　　] the store to be busy, but there are not many customers. He explains that the store is in a business district, so it is not very busy on weekends. Laura hasn't eaten breakfast, so she [3　　　　　　　　] two donuts and a cup of coffee. They [4　　　　　　　] to hang out in the evening after he finishes work.

visits	buys	expects	decide

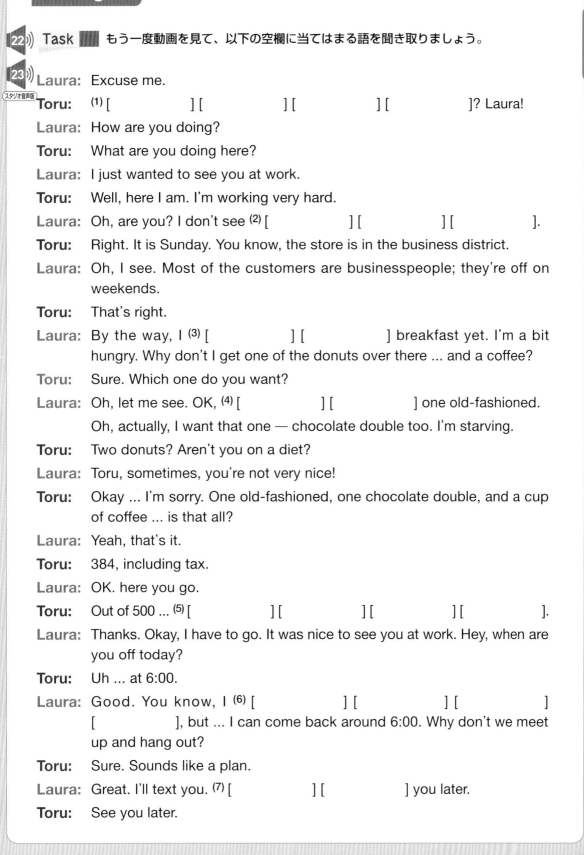

Dialogue

23))) **Laura:** Excuse me.

Toru: (1) [   ] [   ] [   ] [   ]? Laura!

Laura: How are you doing?

Toru: What are you doing here?

Laura: I just wanted to see you at work.

Toru: Well, here I am. I'm working very hard.

Laura: Oh, are you? I don't see (2) [   ] [   ] [   ].

Toru: Right. It is Sunday. You know, the store is in the business district.

Laura: Oh, I see. Most of the customers are businesspeople; they're off on weekends.

Toru: That's right.

Laura: By the way, I (3) [   ] [   ] breakfast yet. I'm a bit hungry. Why don't I get one of the donuts over there ... and a coffee?

Toru: Sure. Which one do you want?

Laura: Oh, let me see. OK, (4) [   ] [   ] one old-fashioned. Oh, actually, I want that one — chocolate double too. I'm starving.

Toru: Two donuts? Aren't you on a diet?

Laura: Toru, sometimes, you're not very nice!

Toru: Okay ... I'm sorry. One old-fashioned, one chocolate double, and a cup of coffee ... is that all?

Laura: Yeah, that's it.

Toru: 384, including tax.

Laura: OK. here you go.

Toru: Out of 500 ... (5) [   ] [   ] [   ] [   ].

Laura: Thanks. Okay, I have to go. It was nice to see you at work. Hey, when are you off today?

Toru: Uh ... at 6:00.

Laura: Good. You know, I (6) [   ] [   ] [   ] [   ], but ... I can come back around 6:00. Why don't we meet up and hang out?

Toru: Sure. Sounds like a plan.

Laura: Great. I'll text you. (7) [   ] [   ] you later.

Toru: See you later.

Task ▓▓ 語句を並べ替えて、アルバイト先で使える表現を英語で書きましょう。

※文頭の語句も、選択肢の中では小文字で記しています。

1. 何かお探しですか？

   Are [looking for / you / something]?

α	だれが	する（です）	だれ・なに	どこ	いつ
Are					

2. すぐにお持ちしますね。

   [will bring / it / right away / I].

だれが	する（です）	だれ・なに	どこ	いつ

3. 申し訳ありませんが、その商品はここに置いてないんです。

   [don't have / we / the item / here / afraid].

だれが	する（です）	だれ・なに	どこ	いつ
I	am			

4. 袋は必要ですか？

   Do [need / you / a bag]?

α	だれが	する（です）	だれ・なに	どこ	いつ
Do					

It's Your Turn!

こんな時、あなたならどうする？

大学生の中には、アルバイトで英語を使う機会がある人も多いようです。ここでは、role play を通して、アルバイト先で使える英語を練習しましょう。

Task ▓ Dealing with Customers

Q. ペアになり、深夜のコンビニの店員（cashier）とお客さん（customer）の役を決めましょう。あいにくお客さんは英語しか話せません。以下の状況で、うまくコミュニケーションがとれますか？

Situation 1

Customer

・所持金 1,000 円（1,000 円札 1 枚）
・通常サイズのアイスコーヒーが欲しい
・3 日前に日本に来たばかりのアメリカ人

Cashier

・アイスコーヒーは、通常（medium, 100 円）と大きめ（large, 130 円）のサイズがある
・コーヒーは機械からのセルフサービス
・どこの国から来たかを尋ね、少し会話をしたい

Situation 2

Customer

・所持金 300 円
・チョコドーナッツ（120 円）が二つ欲しい
・今アルバイトを探していて、自分もここで働けるかを尋ねたい
・来週の予定は特にない

Cashier

・正確にお釣りを渡す
・今バイトの数は足りているが、店長に聞いてみると伝える
・来週の同じ時間に店に来られるかを尋ねる

 Sample Response

必要に応じて会話例を聞くことができます。

Task ▮▮▮ 以下の文章を読んで、設問に答えましょう。

Working Online

Technology has advanced a lot in the 21st century, and lifestyles have changed with it. This includes the ways in which people work. If you have internet access and a laptop or smartphone, it is now possible to work from anywhere in the world. Working online means that you don't have to stay in one location to earn a living. Depending on your work, this could also mean that you will have a flexible work schedule. Many full-time students now also earn money online. There are many kinds of jobs available. You could become an online tutor and teach via video meetings. There are many kinds of proofreading and editing work that you can do online, too. If you have specific skills, there are jobs in translation, graphic design, video-editing, and photography, just to name a few examples. You could become a social media influencer, too. The possibilities are endless. With technology, the future of work will continue to change.

1) According to the passage, how has technology changed the way people work?
   (A) People can now work from anywhere.
   (B) People can earn more money.
   (C) Social media influencers are more popular.
   (D) More and more students take classes online.

2) According to the passage, what is NOT true about working online?
   (A) Many kinds of jobs are available.
   (B) Your work schedule is often flexible.
   (C) The possibilities are endless.
   (D) You do not need any specific skills.

3) Would you be interested in working online? Why, or why not?

Shopping at a Clothing Shop

Unit 13 に続いて、買い物をするとき・接客する
ときの基本的な表現を学びましょう。

Target 買い物で使える英語表現

Watching the Video Clip (1st time)

Task 動画を見た後、以下の問いに答えましょう。

Q. Which of the following sentences is true?

(A) The store clerk gives Laura the wrong change.

(B) Laura asks the store clerk for discounts.

(C) There is good customer service for foreigners.　　　　(　　　　　)

 26 ## Words & Expressions

Task イラストを見て、フレーズを完成させましょう。

1.

このジャケットを試着してもいいですか？
Can I (t　　　　　) this jacket
(o　　　　　)?

2.

このTシャツはいくらですか？
(H　　　　　) (m　　　　　) is this
T-shirt?

3.

どう、似合ってる？
How do I (l　　　　　)?

4.

これらのアクセサリーは高いです。
(T　　　　　) (a　　　　　) are
very pricey.

Task 🔳 もう一度動画を見て、以下の問いに答えましょう。

Q1. ストーリーに沿った正しい順番に並べなさい。

(A) Laura tries a jacket on in the fitting room.

(B) Laura is concerned about the size.

(C) Laura decides to pay by cash.

(　　　　　) → (　　　　　) → (　　　　　)

Q2. How much is the jacket that Laura buys?

It is _____ yen.

Summary

Task 🔳 選択肢から適切な単語を選び、Summary を完成させましょう。

Summary of the Dialogue

While visiting *Amemura* in Osaka, Toru and Laura decide to [1　　　　　　　] out the shops. When Laura goes into a vintage clothing shop, she is [2　　　　　　　　] to find that the clerk is able to speak English. When she finds a cute jacket, Toru suggests that she try it on. He tells her that it really [3　　　　　　　　] her. Laura wants to ask the clerk to lower the price since the jacket is a bit expensive, but Toru says this shop probably does not give [4　　　　　　　].

check	discounts	surprised	suits

Dialogue

 Task もう一度動画を見て、以下の空欄に当てはまる語を聞き取りましょう。

Toru: This is Amemura.

Laura: (1) [   ] [   ] "American Village," right? Why do you call it that?

Toru: Good question. I don't know the answer, though. Actually, this is my first time coming here, too.

Laura: Oh, is it? We should check it out together then.

Toru: Sure, why don't we (2) [   ] [   ] the second-hand clothing shop over there?

Laura: Let's do that. I love vintage clothes!

Clerk: Hello, may I help you?

Laura: Oh, we're (3) [   ] [   ].

Clerk: Sure. Let me know if you have any questions.

Laura: Thanks. Will do.

Clerk: Enjoy shopping.

Laura: Oh, the clerk just (4) [   ] [   ] me in English. That's so cool.

Toru: Probably they have customers from outside Japan, so some staff can speak English. I guess they have some who can speak Chinese, too.

Laura: Oh, I see. Oh, this is so cute, but I wonder if it's the right size.

Toru: Why don't you (5) [   ] [   ] [   ]? There is a fitting room over there.

Laura: Sounds like a good idea. Give me a few minutes, please.

Toru: No problem.

Laura: (6) [   ] [   ] [   ] [   ]?

Toru: You look great. It really suits you.

Laura: Thanks. But it's a bit too pricey. Do you think that the clerk will lower the price for me? I heard that people in Osaka don't hesitate to ask for discounts. What's the word ... oh, "Makete!"

Toru: You know that very well! Right, some shops around here might (7) [   ] [   ] a discount, but I don't think this shop will.

Laura: Oh, I see. I'll try another time.

Toru: Yeah, but do you know why people in Osaka negotiate prices?

Laura: Because they love money?

Toru: Definitely, but they also do it because they like to talk.

Laura: Oh, I see. I like that!

Clerk: How would you like to pay—cash or credit card?

Laura: Cash, please.

Clerk: That'll be 8,640 yen please.

Laura: OK.

Clerk: All right. Here's your change.

Laura: Thanks.

Clerk: Have a nice day.

Laura: Thanks. You too.

Task ▓▓ 語句を並べ替えて、買い物で使える表現を英語で書きましょう。

※文頭の語句も、選択肢の中では小文字で記しています。

1. もう少し小さいサイズはありますか？

   Do [have / you / a smaller size]?

α	だれが	する（です）	だれ・なに	どこ	いつ
Do					

2. この商品の中でオススメはありますか？

   What do [among these items / recommend / you]?

α	だれが	する（です）	だれ・なに	どこ	いつ
What do					

3. これ２つください。

   [would like / I / two of these].

だれが	する（です）	だれ・なに	どこ	いつ

4. レシートもらえますか？

   Could [get / I / a receipt]?

α	だれが	する（です）	だれ・なに	どこ	いつ
Could					

It's Your Turn!

こんな時、あなたならどうする？

どんな国を訪れても、買い物で使える言葉を知っていると重宝します。ここでは、role play を通して、服を買う際に使う英語を練習してみましょう。

Task ▓ Buying What You Want

Q. ペアになり、アパレルのショップ店員（shop clerk）とお客さん（customer）の役を決めましょう。ショップ店員は英語しか話せません。以下の状況で、あなたの欲しいものが買えますか？

Situation 1

Customer
・所持金80ドル、カードは不携帯
・キャップが欲しい
・別の色があるかを尋ねたい。もしなければ黄色を買う。

Shop clerk
・キャップは税込み52ドル
・別の色のキャップはない
・サングラス（35ドル）も勧める

Situation 2

Customer
・現金なし、カードのみ
・Tシャツが欲しい
・試着してから買いたい
・試着後、一つ小さいサイズがあるか尋ねる

Shop clerk
・Tシャツは税込み35ドル
・カード払いOK
・試着室は2階（今は1階にいる）
・Tシャツの在庫は十分

 Sample Response

必要に応じて会話例を聞くことができます。

Read, Think, and Write

🔊 Task ▊▊▊ 以下の文章を読んで、設問に答えましょう。

Vintage Clothing

Many people enjoy wearing vintage clothing. Vintage clothing can make your fashion style unique because there are various styles that you will not find in regular clothing stores. There are many places where you can buy vintage clothing including online stores. From independent shops to flea markets, if you look carefully, you will be able to find good quality clothes from many different eras.

Vintage clothing might look stylish and fashionable, but that is not all. When you wear vintage clothing, you not only reuse clothes but you reduce waste, too. By wearing vintage clothing, you could say that you are helping the world become cleaner! Also, if you have any clothes that you don't wear anymore, you can consider giving them to somebody or selling the clothes instead of throwing them away. You can also donate clothes to different organizations such as NGOs and local recycling centers. Wearing vintage clothing is a sustainable choice for a lot of people who love fashion.

1) According to the passage, where is vintage clothing NOT found?
   (A) At flea markets
   (B) In independent shops
   (C) In regular clothing stores
   (D) At online stores

2) What are you encouraged to do with clothes that you don't wear any more?
   (A) Throw them away
   (B) Donate them to an organization
   (C) Start an online store
   (D) Buy other clothes

3) Do you like wearing vintage clothes? Why, or why not?

Unit 15

Asakusa

Toru は Laura に浅草の観光案内をします。Toru がどのように街や日本的な事柄を説明しているのかを学びましょう。

Target オススメの場所を紹介する英語表現

Watching the Video Clip (1st time)

Task 動画を見た後、以下の問いに答えましょう。

Q. Which of the following sentences is NOT true?

(A) Laura likes *ningyo-yaki* with sweet bean paste.
(B) Toru pays 300 yen for Laura's snack.
(C) Toru recommends that Laura buy *ningyo-yaki*. (　　　　)

31

Words & Expressions

Task イラストを見て、フレーズを完成させましょう。

1.

ここは日本でいちばん有名な観光スポットです。

This is the most famous (t　　　　　) spot in Japan.

2.

ここで沢山の伝統品や可愛いお土産を見つけることが出来ます。

I can find many (t　　　　　) goods and cute souvenirs here.

3.

すみません、あのお寺と一緒に写真を撮ってもらっていいですか？

Excuse me. Could you (t　　　　　) a picture of us with that temple?

4.

建物の中を見学することをお勧めします。

I (r　　　　　) you look inside of the building.

Task ▓ もう一度動画を見て、以下の問いに答えましょう。

Q1. ストーリーに沿った正しい順番に並べなさい。

    (A)   Laura can't read what is written on the big lantern.

    (B)   Laura and Toru fan smoke over their heads.

    (C)   Laura says her image of Tokyo is similar to her image of New York.

                     (   ) → (   ) → (   )

Q2. Why does Laura feel differently when she sees the souvenir stores?

    (A)   Because *Kaminarimon* is one of the popular tourist spots in Japan

    (B)   Because Laura's image of Tokyo was like New York

    (C)   Because Laura and Toru fan smoke over their heads at *Sensouji* temple

                                               (   )

Summary

Task ▓ 選択肢から適切な単語を選び、Summary を完成させましょう。

Summary of the Dialogue

Laura and Toru are [¹   ] in Asakusa, and Laura is surprised by its old-fashioned atmosphere. To her, Tokyo is a big modern city like New York. Toru tells her there are a lot of interesting things to buy in Asakusa, such as old-fashion toys and traditional snacks. Laura gets excited and says she will recommend this place to her friends when they come to Japan. Toru [²   ] Laura to *ningyo-yaki*, and then they [³   ] *Sensoji* Temple and [⁴   ] smoke over their heads.

sightseeing	visit	introduces	fan

Dialogue

 Task もう一度動画を見て、以下の空欄に当てはまる語を聞き取りましょう。

Laura: Oh look ... there's a large lantern over there. What do the letters on it read?

Toru: It reads *Kaminarimon*. It literally means "Thunder Gate." As you can see, it is a gate.

Laura: Really? Is this place famous?

Toru: Yeah. Actually, this is one of the (1) [   ] [   ] [   ] spots in Japan. See, there are a lot of souvenir shops lined up here.

Laura: Oh, this place is a bit different.

Toru: Different from what?

Laura: I mean ... from other parts of Tokyo. My image of Tokyo has always been (2) [   ] [   ], [   ] city ... like New York, in the U.S. In this part of town, however, some bits of old Japan seem to be left.

Toru: You are right. Some elements of old Japanese culture remain in Asakusa.

Laura: Wow! I can find a lot of cool stuff here.

Toru: Right. The things found here are never tiring. Some stores sell (3) [   ] [   ] to foreign travelers, while in other stores you can find old fashioned toys, traditional snacks, and so on.

Laura: Awesome! I'll definitely tell my friends in America to come to this place when they visit Japan.

Toru: That sounds like a good idea. Hey, would you like to try a snack famous in Asakusa?

Laura: Sure. What kind of snack?

Toru: (4) [   ] [   ] this.

Laura: What's that?

Toru: It is a kind of cake. It is shaped like a doll. We call it *ningyo-yaki*.

Laura: It looks like a pancake. Okay, I'll buy this one.

Toru: Well, you can taste it before you buy. Also, there are two kinds, one with the sweet bean paste in it, and one without.

Laura: Okay, (5) [   ] [   ] them first. Oh, that's really good. I like the one with the sweet beans. Hmm ... I'm going to buy some.

Toru: Okay, I can pay for you. How many would you like?

Laura: Well, how much is it for one with sweet beans?

Toru: It's 300 yen for 4, and 500 yen for 8.

Laura: I'll take 8.

Toru: Okay, give me a second. I'll (6) [   ] [   ] [   ] them.

Laura: Wow! What is over there?

Toru: *Sensoji* Temple. It's a temple where people go to receive blessings.

Laura: I know it's a temple. But ... what are those people doing?

Toru: They are bathing themselves in the smoke. It is said that, if your head is exposed to the smoke, you will (7) [   ] [   ] [   ].

Laura: Oh, really? It's interesting.

Toru: Why don't we try it?

Laura: Sure. Let's give it a shot.

Task 語句を並べ替えて、オススメの場所を紹介する際に使える表現を英語で書きましょう。

※文頭の語句も、選択肢の中では小文字で記しています。

1. この場所をオススメする理由は三つです。

[three reasons / this place / recommend / to you / I].

α	だれが	する（です）	だれ・なに	どこ	いつ
	I	have			
(why)					

2. その美術館までは、約一時間半かかります。

[about one and a half hours / to the museum / to get].

だれが	する（です）	だれ・なに	どこ	いつ
It	takes			

3. そのテーマパークなら一日中楽しめますよ。

[at the theme park / can enjoy / you / a whole day].

だれが	する（です）	だれ・なに	どこ	いつ

4. ぜひまたすぐにそこに行きたいです。

[again soon / there / I / would love to go].

だれが	する（です）	だれ・なに	どこ	いつ

It's Your Turn!

こんな時、あなたならどうする？

自分をアピールすることは、海外の人とコミュニケーションをとる上で大切なことです。ここでは、オススメの観光スポットの紹介を通して、自分のアピール力を鍛えましょう。

Task ▓ **Recommending a Sightseeing Spot**

Q1. 海外からの観光客にオススメの観光スポットを、<u>1分間</u>で紹介する準備をしましょう。

> Note.

Q2. 4人グループの中でそれぞれ1分間ずつ話し、グループ内での1番のオススメスポットを決めましょう。

Q3. グループの代表者がそれぞれ1分間ずつ話し、クラス全体での1番のオススメスポットを決めましょう。

 34))

Sample Response

必要に応じて会話例を聞くことができます。

Task 以下の文章を読んで、設問に答えましょう。

Travel Writing

There are many good books about traveling in Japan. For example, if you are interested in history and traditional ways of life, you could read about journeys along ancient Buddhist paths. If you want to know more about contemporary Japan, you could read city travel guides that introduce readers to interesting places, such as cafés, amusement parks, and museums. It is not always easy to travel, even in your own country. When it is difficult to travel, you can read travel literature. Books about traveling allow you to dream about where you want to go some day and make plans for your next trip. Travel literature can also help your imagination so that you can travel in your mind! When you read books about your own culture and home country, you may gain new perspectives about where you are from. You might even make new discoveries, not only about your own country, but also about yourself.

1) According to the passage, what can readers do after reading city travel guides?
   (A) Learn about history
   (B) Inspire other people's imagination
   (C) Find interesting places
   (D) Know more about yourself

2) What is NOT true about travel literature?
   (A) It might help you gain new perspectives about your home country.
   (B) It can help you make plans for your next trip.
   (C) It can help you travel in your mind.
   (D) It can help you learn foreign larguages.

3) What part of Japanese culture would you like to introduce to the world?

Pronunciation

Consonants 1（子音 1）

 /b/, /v/ の違い

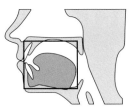

/b/

上下の唇を結んだ状態から一気に破裂させるように離して音を出します。

/v/

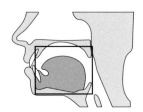

上の歯を下唇に当て、その間からこするように音を出します。

▶ /b/, /v/ を使った表現を聞き、発音してみましょう。

- **b**ring their local food
- **b**y the way
- That'd **b**e great.

- ha**v**e fun o**v**er a **v**ariety of food
- in**v**ite them
- I ha**v**en't decided yet

 /f/, /h/ の違い

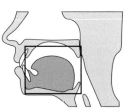

/f/

/v/ と同じように上の歯を下唇に当て、そのすき間から声を出さずに息を送ります。

/h/

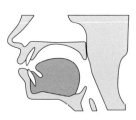

喉の奥にある声門をこするように息をハーッと吐き出します。

▶ /f/, /h/ を使った表現を聞き、発音してみましょう。

- **f**ind a crosswalk
- go straight **f**or a while
- **f**ollow me

- **h**ow to get there
- walk over the **h**ill

/ð/, /z/ の違い

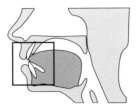 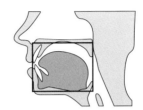

/ð/	/z/
舌の先を歯の間から突き出して音を出します。	上の歯茎に舌の先を近づけて音を出します。

▶ /ð/, /z/ を使った表現を聞き、発音してみましょう。

- **th**is morning
- lived in **the** United States
- take you **th**ere

- My name i**s** Toru Asano.
- I wa**s** born and grew up in Tokyo.
- It say**s** Building 8.

  /θ/, /s/ の違い

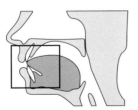 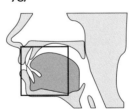

/θ/	/s/
口の形は /ð/ と同じですが、音は出しません。舌の先を歯の間から突き出して息を出します。	口の形は /z/ と同じですが、音は出しません。上の歯茎に舌の先を近づけて息を出します。

▶ /θ/, /s/ を使った表現を聞き、発音してみましょう。

- find every**th**ing okay
- I'm **th**inking.
- **th**anks a lot

- a profe**ss**or at this univer**s**ity
- **s**pend a lot of time
- **s**tudy at the library

Consonants 2 (子音 2)

  /r/, /l/ の違い

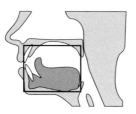
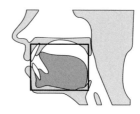

/r/
下の先を歯茎につけない程度に巻き上げます。また唇を少し丸めます。

/l/
上の歯茎に舌の先をくっつけて息を出します。

▶ /r/, /l/ を使った表現を聞き、発音してみましょう。

- ・remember me
- ・on the train
- ・from the station

- ・Hello, Laura!
- ・She helps me a lot.
- ・I know how you feel.

  /m/, /n/ の違い

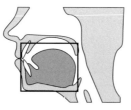
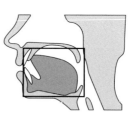

/m/
唇を閉じて息を鼻から出して音を出します。/mu/のように余計な母音を後につけないように注意してください。

/n/
/l/ と似ていますが、舌先及び舌の両側を歯茎に押し付けるようにして鼻から音を出します。

▶ /m/, /n/ を使った表現を聞き、発音してみましょう。

- ・for a minute
- ・my name is
- ・really like them

- ・today's lesson
- ・interested in the content
- ・in the next class

/tʃ/, /t/ の違い

Point

/tʃ/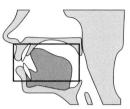

唇を突き出し、舌先及び側面を歯茎につけて、ゆっくりと離すときにこすれることで音を出します。

/t/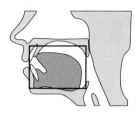

唇を突き出し、舌先及び側面を歯茎につけて、すぐに離します。

▶ /tʃ/, /t/ を使った表現を聞き、発音してみましょう。

- decide whi**ch** classes
- a lot of **ch**oices
- Japanese pop cul**t**ure

- **t**ake his class
- only **t**wo elec**t**ives

  /g/, /ŋ/ の違い

Point

/g/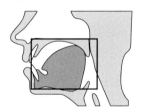

舌の奥の部分を上に持ち上げて、上顎の奥、喉の前の柔らかい部分に押し付けるようにして発音します。

/ŋ/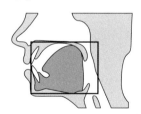

舌の奥の部分を持ち上げて、上の顎につけるのはほぼ /g/ と同じですが、鼻から息を出して音を作ります。

▶ /g/, /ŋ/ を使った表現を聞き、発音してみましょう。

- a bi**g** deal
- That's **g**ood to hear.
- sunny-side-up e**gg**s

- How's school goi**ng**?
- do the same thi**ng**
- I love cooki**ng**.

97

Pronunciation

Vowels & Diphthongs（母音・二重母音）

44 》 母音（vowels）

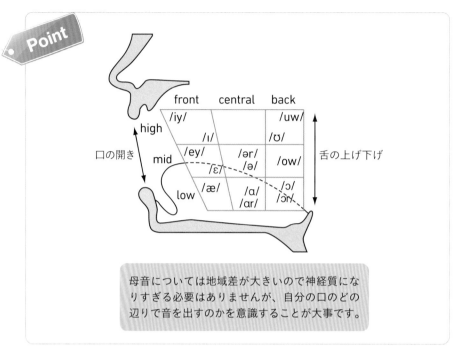

Point

母音については地域差が大きいので神経質になりすぎる必要はありませんが、自分の口のどの辺りで音を出すのかを意識することが大事です。

▶ 下線部の母音を意識して聞き、自分でも発音してみましょう。

C**a**n y**ou** h**e**lp m**e** out?
/æ/ /uw/ /ɛ/　/iy/

W**ou**ld **i**t be ok**ay**?
/ʊ/　/ɪ/ /iy/　/ey/

res**e**rve t**i**ck**e**ts
/ɪ/ /ər/　/ɪ/　/ɛ/

pr**o**b**a**bly c**o**sts **a**bout t**e**n thous**a**nd y**e**n
/ɑ/ /ə/　/ɔ/　/ə/　　/ɛ/　　/ə/　/ɛ/

g**o**ing al**o**ne
/ow/　　/ow/

C**ou**ld you **or**der one for m**e**?
/ʊ/　　　/ɔr/　　　　/iy/

p**ar**ked my c**ar** b**e**hind **a** tr**u**ck
/ɑr/　　　/ɑr/ /iy/　/ə/ /ʌ/

二重母音（diphthongs）

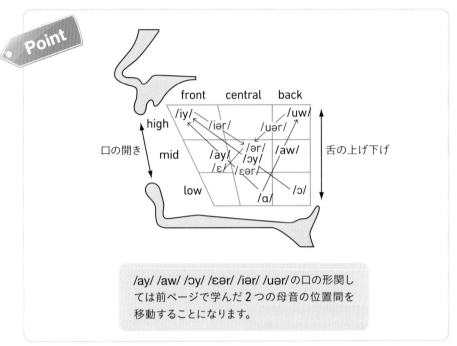

/ay/ /aw/ /ɔy/ /ɛər/ /iər/ /uər/の口の形関しては前ページで学んだ2つの母音の位置間を移動することになります。

▶下線部の二重母音を意識して聞き、自分でも発音してみましょう。

in m**y** hromet**ow**n
　　/ay/　　/aw/

Are th**ere** any t**oy** stores around h**ere**?
　　/ɛər/　　/ɔy/　　　　　　/iər/

gave a p**oor** performance last year
　　　　/uər/

Stress & Rhythm （強勢・リズム）

  語内の強勢（word stress）

> **Point** 各単語内の強勢がある箇所は、強く、長く、はっきりと発音されます。逆に、強勢のない箇所は、弱く、短く発音されます。

▶次の単語内の強勢がある位置に注意して聞き、自分でも発音してみましょう。

- quéstion
- ánswer
- togéther
- víntage
- cústomer

- mínutes
- hésitate
- rècomménd
- anóther
- negòtiátion

  文内の強勢（sentence stress）

> **Point** それぞれの文において大事な情報は他の部分に比べて、強く、長く、はっきりと発音されます。

▶囲んである部分を中心に文内の強勢に注意して聞き、自分でも発音してみましょう。

Would you like something to drink ?

Why don't we go to a tea house ?

Green tea is a bitter drink.

I want to drink real green tea.

It tastes like medicine .

Point 英語は強勢のある音節以外は速く発音され、強勢のある音節どうし の間隔は通常ほぼ同じ長さになります。

▶ リズムを意識しながら音声を聞き、手を叩きながら発音してみましょう。

Melissa makes coffee.

Melissa is making some coffee.

Melissa will make some coffee.

Melissa likes to make some coffee.

Melissa has made some coffee.

▶ リズムを意識しながら音声を聞き、発音してみましょう。

I'm working very hard.

Most of the customers are businesspeople.

You're not very nice.

When are you off today?

ようこそ! ニッポンへ ［改訂版］
─映像で学ぶ大学基礎英語 留学生の日本文化体験─

検印省略	©2022 年 1 月 31 日　第 1 版発行
	2023 年 1 月 31 日　第 2 刷発行

監修　　　　　　　　　　田地野　彰

編著　　　　　　　　　　石井　洋佑

　　　　　　　　　　　　加藤　由崇

　　　　　　　　　　　　中川　　浩

発行者　　　　　　　　　原　雅久

発行所　　　　　　株式会社 朝日出版社
〒101-0065 東京都千代田区西神田 3-3-5
電話　東京　(03) 3239-0271
FAX　東京　(03) 3239-0479
E-mail　text-e@asahipress.com
振替口座　00140-2-46008
http://www.asahipress.com/
組版／メディアアート　製版／図書印刷

乱丁・落丁本はお取り替えいたします。
ISBN 978-4-255-15682-8